THE
FILMS
OF
BETTE DAVIS

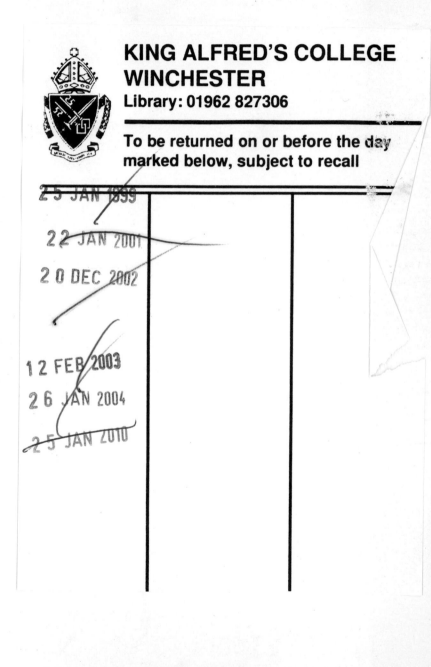

THE
FILMS
OF
BETTE DAVIS

by Gene Ringgold

The Citadel Press   New York

SECOND PAPERBOUND EDITION, 1971

Copyright © 1966 by Gene Ringgold

Published by The Citadel Press,
222 Park Avenue South, New York, N. Y. 10003

In Canada: George J. McLeod Ltd., 73 Bathurst St.,
Toronto 2B, Ontario

Printed in the United States of America by
Noble Offset Printers, Inc., New York, N. Y.

Library of Congress Catalog Card No.: 66-11041
SBN 8065-0000-X

Designed by Martin Fuller

Photograph Acknowledgments:

Carlos Clarens, Homer Dickens, Embassy Pictures,
Weimer Gard, Clyde Jump, Albert Lord, Gunnard
Nelson, Paramount Pictures, Inc., Romano Tozzi,
Twentieth Century-Fox Pictures, Inc., Warner
Brothers Pictures, Inc.

Special thanks to
Mrs. Lillian Schwartz and her staff at the library
of the Academy of Motion Picture Arts and
Sciences for their invaluable assistance.

CONTENTS

FOREWORD
by Henry Hart

Critics and others who have studied the acting art say there are two kinds of successful actors and actresses: those who project by craftsmanship an image to which the public reacts favorably, and those who project such an image by the sheer force of personality.

Like most generalities, this one is not true in all cases, but in the case of Bette Davis it is doubly true. She succeeded at first by projecting an image which was the essence of personality, and has survived as a star because she was sufficiently intelligent and hard-working to learn the acting craft.

This sequence of personality first and craftsmanship later is the usual one and many actresses, if their careers continue into middle age and beyond, owe their professional longevity to the luck, ambition, or whatever which induced them to master their craft. On the stage, and certainly on the screen, art *does* improve on nature.

A player can have both craft and personality, however, and still not become a star of the first magnitude for, unless he or she be an artist of considerable range, the image he or she most often projects, and the one by which he or she is identified in the public mind, must conform to what the Germans call *Zeitgeist*, or some part thereof.

Unfortunately, no English word fully expresses all the ideas *Zeitgeist* was designed to convey. "The spirit of the times" is the usual translation, but "spirit" is ambiguous and "of the times" imprecise. Philosophically, *Zeitgeist* means the totality of significant trends—cultural, moral, economic and political—in a particular place at a particular time. Even finished actors and actresses can fail to reach the heights because they are intellectually, temperamentally or politically out of sympathy, or phase, with the *Zeitgeist* prevailing in the nation, or region, in which they perform. And, when the *Zeitgeist* changes, stars who do not change decline and fall.

The part of our *Zeitgeist* which Miss Davis' screen image subserved is feminism.

Which is not to say that Miss Davis' films have been overt feminist propaganda. What is meant is this: in her every role audiences sensed an exemplar of "the new woman." The result was women had a double pleasure watching her since, in addition to a good acting performance, they saw one of their own confront the male with a new independence, as well as with the immemorial web.

Why did men like her? I am not sure they did, *really*. Men are notorious for being fascinated by those women who have their interests least at heart. Some men enjoy observing a woman they think might be hard to master—stalking her, learning which doors are locked and which windows unlatched. Some knowing men of my acquaintance enjoyed watching the phenomenon of Bette Davis herself—a not especially good-looking girl, slightly exophthalmic in fact—getting away with an arrogance that had *what* to back it up?

The "what" is described very differently by Miss Davis' admirers and detractors. The latter are voluble about her having been reared and driven by an ambitious and man-hating mother; about her "masculine protest"; about, in fact, almost everything except the things Miss Davis' admirers emphasize—intelligence, self-discipline, capacity for hard work and, above all, ambition.

I am not at all sure one can divine anything truly objective about an actress' private psyche from the roles she elects to play or is chosen for. It's possible, however, and it certainly is not without significance that Miss Davis' first important success was as Mildred in *Of Human Bondage* and that she now appears in "horror" films like *What Ever Happened to Baby Jane?* and *Hush . . . Hush, Sweet Charlotte.*

If you think it *is* possible to find the real Bette Davis among the disparate people she has portrayed on the screen I suggest that you pass over *Juarez, The Old Maid, The Private Lives of Elizabeth and Essex, The Letter, The Little Foxes* and *All About Eve,* and study her performance in a recent soap opera.

The *grande dame* Miss Davis portrays in *Where Love Has Gone* is the way *grandes dames* should be in real life. And the kind of *grande dame* Miss Davis should have been.

THE
FILMS
OF
BETTE DAVIS

Part One:
APPRENTICESHIP

The career of Bette Davis has been a distinguished one. Her contributions to motion pictures are even more impressive when consideration is given to the personal misfortunes and professional disappointments which profoundly affected her life but were never severe enough to frustrate her determination to become an actress and a great film star. Her detractors, believing her acting ability is subservient to her electric personality, reluctantly admit that her skill as a performer is so artful she has advanced feminism on the screen to a zenith where many men, as well as most women, find her fascinating.

Part of this fatal fascination is the phenomenon of seeing a genuine realist performing her job so well she has occasionally been able to make the most mediocre Hollywood fantasy seem intelligent. Her ambition, will power and mastery of her craft, combined with an old-fashioned intelligence we once called "common horse sense," are the vital components of a screen image unique enough to survive three decades of social and economic evolutions.

An esteemed critic, who once admitted an averse admiration for Bette Davis, theorized that she would have been burned as a witch if she had been born in Lowell, Massachusetts, two hundred years ago instead of April 5, 1908. Another admirer, ruminating recently on television about what might have happened if she had sought a political career, concluded she would probably have been the first woman elected President of the United States.

Her parents were incompatible and they divorced while she was still quite young. Supposedly, this affected her psychology to where she later believed it was more important for her to concentrate on a career than on domesticity. Her own marital record, once widowed, thrice divorced, substantiates that being the child of a broken marriage had traumatic consequences. So do the roles she sought to play in motion pictures. Those which brought her the greatest acclaim have all been variations of the free-thinking, emancipated woman. Seldom has she successfully essayed a portrait of a happily married wife, a contented mother or a deeply religious woman with divine beliefs. It is curious that during her varied career, she never played a nun on the screen. This is an ideal characterization for a dedicated and accomplished actress to undertake and Miss Davis might be wise to give consideration to such a role. The results should be gratifying as well as interesting.

While in her freshman year at high school, Bette Davis abandoned her ideas of becoming a dancer in favor of an acting career. Once her mind was made up, she acted in school productions, with summer stock companies and semiprofessional groups. After Eva LeGallienne rejected her as a drama student, she attended classes at John Murray Anderson's acting school. A role with the Provincetown Players in an off-Broadway production of *The Earth Between*, in 1928, was followed by a part in *The Wild Duck* with a touring repertory company. In No-

11

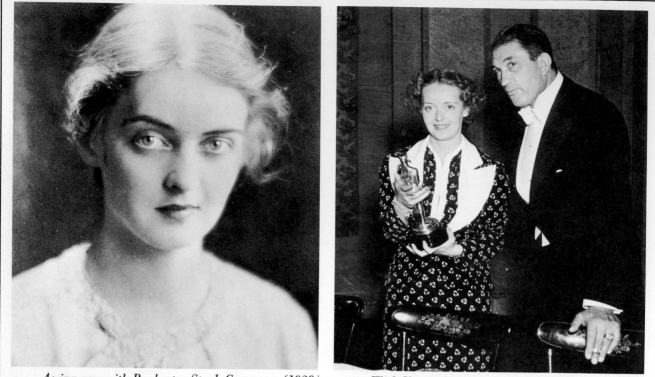

As ingenue with Rochester Stock Company (1928)   With Victor McLaglen at 1935 Academy Awards

vember of 1929, she made her Broadway debut in Martin Flavin's domestic comedy, *Broken Dishes*. Early the following year, she flubbed a screen test for Samuel Goldwyn. Her last Broadway appearance before her film career was in *Solid South*, which opened in October of 1930 and closed within three weeks. She did not appear again on the New York stage until 1952 when she starred in *Two's Company*, a musical revue lasting less than ninety performances. Her only other Broadway appearances were as Maxine Falk in Tennessee Williams' *The Night of the Iguana*, in 1961, and a short-lived evening of recitations called *The World of Carl Sandburg*.

A screen test, arranged for her by David Werner, a talent scout for Universal Pictures, resulted in her being signed by that studio to a six-month contract. Late in 1930 Bette Davis, accompanied by her mother, arrived in Hollywood. More than once during her first year there, she thought herself a failure in films. She made three indifferent pictures at her home studio and an equally inconsequential one on loan-out to RKO. Mae Clarke replaced her in what was to have been her fourth Universal film, *Frankenstein*, a harbinger that might well have anticipated that Bette Davis' dowager days in movies would be spent playing the screen's most formidable witch.

In 1932, "the little brown wren" who Carl Laemmle claimed had "as much sex-appeal as Slim Summerville," bleached her hair to a golden blonde and played the ingenue in a George Arliss picture so satisfactorily that a gratified Warner Brothers signed her to a seven-year con-

tract. Four years, and 24 films later, Bette Davis' unconfined joy turned to open rebellion. In an English courtroom, she fought to free herself from her Warner contract and to establish her right to make films she felt were worthy of her fully developed talents. She lost her fight but her argument was in a good cause. Eventually, she won the esteem of Warner Brothers, the admiration of the film industry and the popularity synonymous with being the screen's most important actress.

Although she appeared in 31 films during her apprenticeship, only two of them have historical importance: *Of Human Bondage*, a true cinema classic, contains a Bette Davis performance still alluded to as one of the screen's greatest acting accomplishments; and *Dangerous*, a melodramatic soap opera in which her performance was so good that her peers voted her an Academy Award. Four of her films of this period contained Davis performances worthwhile enough to be favorably remembered: *Cabin in the Cotton*; *Fog Over Frisco*; *Bordertown*; and *The Petrified Forest*.

Two films, also worth mentioning, had a perverse effect on her career. Her disappointment over *not* being cast in *Anthony Adverse* in the role awarded subsequently to Olivia de Havilland and *being* cast in *Satan Met a Lady*, which she considers her all-time worst film, were the factors that motivated her unprecedented rebellion: her flight to England and her ultimate court battle.

All of her apprenticeship films have a nostalgic curiosity to Bette Davis devotees and to all movie buffs addicted enough to be interested in the evolution of sound pictures.

With David Durand in "Bad Sister"

With George Arliss in "The Man Who Played God"

BAD SISTER

A Universal Picture (1931)

Cast Conrad Nagel, Sidney Fox, Bette Davis, ZaSu Pitts, Slim Summerville, Charles Winninger, Emma Dunn, Humphrey Bogart, Bert Roach, David Durand.

Credits Produced by Carl Laemmle, Jr. Directed by Hobart Henley. Screen play by Raymond L. Schrock and Tom Reed. Additional dialogue by Edwin Knopf. Based on *The Flirt* by Booth Tarkington. Photographed by Karl Freund. Edited by Ted Kent. Running time, 68 minutes.

Synopsis Marianne Madison (Sidney Fox), the spoiled daughter of a small-town Indiana merchant (Charles Winninger), is so bored by the charms of her suitors that she falls in love with Valentine Corliss (Humphrey Bogart), an unctuous confidence man in town to swindle local businessmen.

By promising to build a prosperous factory, Valentine dupes Marianne into forging her father's name to a letter of endorsement which he then uses to elicit money from other merchants. Once he has amassed a sizeable amount, he skips town and induces Marianne to elope with him. He deserts her soon afterward, leaving her to repent in a shabby hotel room.

While Marianne is away with Valentine, her sister Laura (Bette Davis), who has confided her innermost desires only to the pages of her diary, reveals to young Dr. Dick Lindley (Conrad Nagel) that she has been in love with him for years, although she knows he loves Marianne.

Sadder and wiser, Marianne returns home admitting that her foolish behavior has almost ruined her life. To avert further scandal, she accepts a proposal of marriage from a wealthy young man (Bert Roach) whom she previously held in amused contempt. Dr. Lindley, aware he had only been infatuated with the flirtatious Marianne, realizes he loves quiet and dependable Laura.

On the strength of her stage performances in *The Wild Duck, Broken Dishes* and *Solid South*, Bette Davis was given a screen test that resulted in a six-month contract with Universal Studios. Plans to star her in Preston Sturges' *Slightly Dishonorable* were abandoned after Carl Laemmle, Jr. met her and exclaimed, "She has about as much sex-appeal as Slim Summerville!" Using her for the contracted six months, Universal cast her in support of Sidney Fox in *Bad Sister*. Miss Fox, another screen newcomer, was awarded the role in Sturges' comedy, originally intended for Davis.

With Humphrey Bogart and Conrad Nagel

With Conrad Nagel

What the critics said about
BAD SISTER

A. D. S. in *The New York Times*:

What starts out to be a homely Hoosier tragedy finishes as a wooden and insecurely presented story of two sisters who should have known better.

The Misses Sidney Fox and Bette Davis, who are not unknown along the Rialto, make their debut in films as Marianne and Laura Madison.

Miss Fox makes a charming Marianne, but her delicate English intonation is sadly out of place in Council City. Miss Davis' interpretation of Laura is too lugubrious and tends to destroy the sympathy the audience is expected to feel for the young woman.

Waly in *Weekly Variety*:

Sidney Fox is restricted to this small-town big-ideal girl and as such is pleasing. Bette Davis holds much promise in her handling of Laura, sweet, simple, and the very essence of repression.

With Sidney Fox

SEED

A Universal Picture (1931)

Cast John Boles, Genevieve Tobin, Lois Wilson, Raymond Hackett, Bette Davis, Frances Dade, ZaSu Pitts, Richard Tucker, Jack Willis, Bill Willis, Don Cox, Dick Winslow, Kenneth Selling, Terry Cox, Helen Parrish, Dickie Moore.

Credits Produced and directed by John M. Stahl. Screen play by Gladys Lehman. Based on a novel by Charles G. Norris. Photographed by Jackson Rose. Edited by Ted Kent. Running time, 96 minutes.

Synopsis Bart Carter (John Boles), a Bliss Publishing Company clerk, writes a novel in which he has great faith, although his wife, Peggy (Lois Wilson), is completely disinterested in anything but her home and their five children. Bart's former girl friend, Mildred (Genevieve Tobin), the Paris manager of the Bliss firm, expresses a desire to read his manuscript during a U.S. visit. He invites her to dinner at his home and afterward reads his incomplete manuscript to her.

With John Boles

Mildred is most enthusiastic. She convinces publisher Bliss (Richard Tucker) he should subsidize Bart until he finishes the book. The novel is published and acclaimed. Bart, having received a large cash advance, asks Peggy for a divorce. Shocked by his request, she heartbrokenly consents to his wishes when she learns he intends marrying Mildred.

Ten years later, Bart Carter, now a celebrated writer, is accused by critics who once championed him of doing inferior work. He has found it necessary to produce potboilers to keep Mildred in luxury. The financial strain has also resulted in his failing to provide for his children.

To bring him to his sense of responsibility, Peggy invites him to visit their almost full-grown children. He admires Margaret (Bette Davis), his lovely daughter, and marvels at how well his four sons have managed to get along without him. He implores Peggy to allow the children to live with Mildred and him. Knowing they have reached the age where a father's guidance is important, she agrees.

Aware that Bart loves his children more than he loves her, Mildred is faced with an uncertain future as the outsider in a family unit she almost destroyed.

Bette Davis' role was so unimportant critics never bothered to comment on her performance, and Universal considered her contribution to *Seed* so negligible her name seldom appeared in advertisements for it. Miss Davis herself often neglects to include it among her screen credits.

What the critics said about
SEED

Mordaunt Hall in *The New York Times:*

It is a lethargic and often dull production, in spite of the good acting by both Genevieve Tobin as Mildred and Miss Wilson as Peggy, ZaSu Pitts as a servant, and passable performances by some other players.

Shan in *Weekly Variety:*

That Universal has succeeded in making an attractive film out of a homely subject of family life and a father's ambitions is due to the intelligent cast selection, acting, and general treatment. Few pictures move with a more even pace.

WATERLOO BRIDGE

A Universal Picture (1931)

Cast Mae Clark, Kent Douglass (Douglass Montgomery), Doris Lloyd, Ethel Griffies, Enid Bennett, Frederick Kerr, Bette Davis, Rita Carlisle.

Credits Produced by Carl Laemmle, Jr. Directed by James Whale. Screen play by Benn W. Levy. Continuity and additional dialogue by Tom Reed. Based on a play by Robert E. Sherwood. Photographed by Arthur Edeson. Edited by James Whale. Running time, 72 minutes.

Synopsis Myra (Mae Clark), a London chorus girl suddenly unemployed by World War I circumstances, is forced into becoming a prostitute. During an air raid she meets Roy Wetherby (Kent Douglass), a Canadian soldier on furlough, who is attracted to her but unaware she is a streetwalker. Roy falls in love, and just before being shipped to the battle front, he proposes that Myra marry him. In love with him, and believing this to be her opportunity to escape her sordid life, she accepts.

They spend their last weekend with Roy's family at their country house. Myra is welcomed by Roy's uncle (Frederick Kerr), an aristocratic but hard-drinking squire forced to retire from Army duty because of his age; Roy's widowed mother (Enid Bennett); and Janet (Bette Davis), his uncomplicated sister, who is thrilled to hear about his engagement.

The weekend is heartwarming for Roy but heartbreaking for Myra, who realizes that she cannot overcome her unsavory past by marriage. After sending Roy back to his regiment believing she will be his bride when he returns, she confesses the truth about herself to his mother.

She returns to London and one night, while walking near Waterloo Bridge, where she first met Roy, she is killed in an air raid.

What the critics said about
WATERLOO BRIDGE

Leo Meehan in *Motion Picture Herald*:

A distinct triumph for Mae Clark and Kent Douglass. Intelligently directed by [James] Whale, they reveal the tender, tragic romance with great feeling and poignancy. . . . Distinctly the direction and the fine performances of Miss Clark and Douglass make this an unusually gripping picture.

Rush in *Weekly Variety*:

Production is of good quality; players are personable, and there are moments when the story has a sympathetic tug. . . . Absence of strong names is against the picture but the supporting cast is first rate. . . . A London air raid sequence is neatly produced.

NOTE: M-G-M remade *Waterloo Bridge* in 1940 and again in 1956, when it was retitled *Gaby*.

With Mae Clarke

With Doris Lloyd, Kent Douglas (Douglass Montgomery), Mae Clarke, and unidentified actor

WAY BACK HOME

A Radio Picture (1932)

Cast Phillips Lord, Effie Palmer, Mrs. Phillips Lord, Bennett Kilpack, Raymond Hunter, Frank Albertson, Bette Davis, Oscar Apfel, Stanley Fields, Dorothy Peterson, Frankie Darro.

Credits Produced by Pandro S. Berman. Directed by William A. Seiter. Screen play by Jane Murfin. Based on radio characters created by Phillips Lord. Photographed by J. Roy Hunt. Musical score by Max Steiner. Art direction by Max Rhee. Running time, 81 minutes.

Synopsis Seth Parker (Phillips Lord), a Maine preacher, dedicates his life to solving his congregation's domestic problems, settling their petty jealousies, and inspiring them to make their small town a haven of neighborliness and good fellowship.

Seth's home is the center of constant activity—songfests, quilting bees, and prayer meetings. Into it comes Robbie Turner (Frankie Darro), a runaway boy whose father, Rube (Stanley Fields), is a troublemaker and drunkard. Seth welcomes Robbie and protects him from his cruel father. After Rube disappears, he intends to keep him and raise him as his own son.

Dissipated and vindictive, Rube returns and tries to intimidate Seth into giving up his son. The boy, terrified of his father, begs Seth to allow him to remain in his home. Seth makes arrangements to adopt him. Frustrated, Rube attempts to kidnap Robbie, and he attacks Mary Lucy (Bette Davis), a neighbor's daughter who is trying

With Stanley Fields

With Frank Albertson

to help the boy she has befriended.

David Clark (Frank Albertson), Mary's boy friend, saves her from Rube, who has taken Robbie away. Seth pursues Rube and intercepts him at the railroad junction. An oncoming train kills Rube as he is trying to elude Seth.

Way Back Home, originally released as *Other People's Business*, was inspired by the popular N.B.C. radio program that starred Phillips Lord, its creator. Bette Davis, loaned to Radio Pictures, completed her scenes and returned to Universal to learn that her short-term contract had not been renewed.

What the critics said about
WAY BACK HOME

Bige in *Weekly Variety:*

The negative or production cost of *Way Back Home* was round $400,000, a lot of coin for a camp meeting on screen. As entertainment, the film is unbelievably bad. The story is strictly an old-style proposed tear-jerker. It runs 81 minutes and seems like 281.

Leo Meehan in *Motion Picture Herald:*

It will bring joy unconfined to Seth Parker's vast radio audience.

THE MENACE

A Columbia Picture (1932)

Cast H. B. Warner, Bette Davis, Walter Byron, Natalie Moorhead, William B. Davidson, Crauford Kent, Halliwell Hobbes, Charles Gerrard, Murray Kinnell.

Credits Produced by Sam Nelson. Directed by Roy William Neil. Screen play by Dorothy Howell and Charles Logue. Dialogue by Roy Chanslor. Based on *The Feathered Serpent* by Edgar Wallace. Photographed by L. William O'Connell. Running time, 64 minutes.

Synopsis Ronald Quayle (Walter Byron), a young Englishman falsely accused and convicted of having murdered his father on the testimony of his stepmother, Caroline (Natalie Moorhead), escapes from prison and flees to the U.S. While he is working in the southwest oil fields, an explosion disfigures his face. Plastic surgery rebuilds his face but alters his appearance. He returns to England, hoping to learn who killed his father, thereby clearing his name.

Posing as Robert Crockett, a prospective buyer for his ancestral estate, which Caroline has put up for sale, he successfully fools Caroline and Peggy (Bette Davis), his *With Walter Byron*

former fiancée, who both fail to recognize him. Convinced Caroline is responsible for his father's death, Ronald wins her confidence through romance.

He presents her with an expensive necklace, which she shows to her other house guests, Utterson (William B. Davidson) and Lewis (Crauford Kent), the men who helped murder her husband. To turn the killers against each other, Ronald steals the necklace back and plants it on Utterson. Lewis finds it and kills Utterson, believing he was attempting to double-cross him. Peggy faints when she discovers the body.

With William B. Davidson, Natalie Moorhead, H. B. Warner, and Halliwell Hobbes

With Walter Byron

Tracy (H. B. Warner), a Scotland Yard inspector, called in to investigate Utterson's murder, immediately realizes that Robert Crockett is really Ronald Quayle. Before Tracy can arrest him, Ronald stages a trap for Lewis, who ultimately confesses that he and Caroline murdered Ronald's father.

Despite having only the nominal feminine lead in *The Menace*, the film eventually proved to be a lucky one for Bette Davis. Murray Kinnell, one of the supporting players and a close friend of George Arliss, was instrumental in getting her an interview with Arliss which led to her being cast in *The Man Who Played God*, a film she regards as the turning point in her Hollywood career.

What the critics said about
THE MENACE

In *Weekly Variety*:

The Menace is just routine melodrama without menace or perceptible suspense. . . . Bette Davis has to take a decided second to Natalie Moorhead as the adventuress who kills her husband and blames it on her stepson.

In *Film Daily*:

Filled with absurd situations so that the fine work of an excellent cast and good direction are discounted.

HELL'S HOUSE

A Capital Films
Exchange Release (1932)

Cast Junior Durkin, Pat O'Brien, Bette Davis, Junior Coughlan, Charley Grapewin, Emma Dunn, James Marcus, Morgan Wallace, Wallis Clark, Hooper Atchley.

Credits Produced by Benjamin F. Zeidman. Directed by Howard Higgins. Screen play by Paul Gangelin and B. Harrison Orkow. Based on a story by Howard Higgins. Photographed by Allen S. Siegel. Edited by Edward Schroeder. Running time, 72 minutes.

Synopsis Jimmy Mason (Junior Durkin), an unemployed teenager, is befriended by Matt Kelly (Pat O'Brien), a small-time racketeer who gives him a job answering his telephone at his bootlegging headquarters. Jimmy, blinded by admiration for Kelly, doesn't realize the bootlegger is really interested in his girl friend, Peggy Gardner (Bette Davis).

When the police raid Kelly's hideout, Jimmy, the only one present, is arrested. In court he refuses to identify Kelly as his employer and after being reprimanded by a stern judge (Wallis Clark), he is sentenced to three years in a state reformatory.

In this cruelly operated institution, the boys suffer mistreatment from a sadistic guard (Hooper Atchley) and an unscrupulous superintendent (James Marcus). Jimmy becomes friendly with Shorty (Junior Coughlan), an inmate with a serious heart ailment. After Shorty's death from mistreatment, a crusading newspaper publisher (Morgan Wallace) campaigns to have conditions improved, but his efforts are thwarted when the staff is alerted to the fact that the school is to be inspected.

After Jimmy's aunt (Emma Dunn) visits him and tells him that Peggy is seeing a good deal of Kelly, Jimmy escapes in a garbage container and goes to Kelly's apartment where he finds Peggy. She tells him her reason for being friendly with Kelly was to try to persuade him to help get Jimmy out of the reform school.

The police trace Jimmy to the apartment, but before they can arrest him, Kelly confesses his guilt and exonerates Jimmy.

With Pat O'Brien and Junior Durkin   *With Pat O'Brien*

With Pat O'Brien

What the critics said about
HELL'S HOUSE

Mordaunt Hall in *The New York Times:*

The attempt to pillory reform schools in *Hell's House* is hardly adult in its attack, but it has a few moderately interesting interludes. There is, however, insufficient detail on the institutions that appeals to the spectators as being presented without prejudice. . . .

The direction of the film is old-fashioned. Pat O'Brien, who acts the role of Kelly, gives a forced performance. Young Durkin's playing is sincere and likewise that of Bette Davis.

Waly in *Weekly Variety:*

This could have been made into a real first-run, class A Feature. As it is, it merits only attention of the lesser second-runs. . . . The theme, which lent itself excellently to being a *Big House* of a boys' state reformatory, projects as having been put together in a slipshod manner.

With Pat O'Brien and Junior Durkin

THE MAN WHO PLAYED GOD

A Warner Brothers Picture (1932)

Cast George Arliss, Violet Heming, Ivan Simpson, Louise Closser Hale, Bette Davis, Donald Cook, Paul Porcasi, Oscar Apfel, William Janney, Grace Durkin, Raymond (Ray) Milland, Dorothy Libaire, Hedda Hopper, André Luget, Charles Evans, Murray Kinnell, Wade Boteler, Alexander Ikonikoff.

Credits Produced by Jack L. Warner. Directed by John Adolphi. Screen play by Julian Josephson and Maude Howell. Adapted from a short story by Gouverneur Morris and the play *The Silent Voice* by Jules Eckert Goodman. Photographed by James Van Trees. Piano solos by Salvatore Santaella. Edited by William Holmes. Running time, 80 minutes.

With George Arliss

With Violet Heming, George Arliss, and Louise Closser Hale

Synopsis When the king of an important European country is prevented from hearing the Paris concert of Montgomery Royale (George Arliss) by motor trouble, the maestro offers to give a private backstage recital for the disappointed monarch. During this performance an anarchist, intending to assassinate the king, explodes a bomb. Everyone but Royale escapes injury. He is deafened by the explosion.

Learning he will never hear again, he returns to New York accompanied by his sister (Louise Closser Hale), a close friend, Mildred (Violet Heming), and Grace, his fiancée (Bette Davis). All are concerned for him. Despondent over his affliction, he is restrained from a suicide attempt by his faithful servant, Battle (Ivan Simpson).

Discovering he can observe the people who wander through nearby Central Park by learning to read lips and "eavesdropping" on their conversations by using binoculars, Royale becomes quite philanthropic, and several unfortunate persons benefit from his anonymous gifts. Taking great pleasure in playing God, his patronizing façade is eventually changed to complete sincerity when he observes Grace tearfully telling Harold, a young man (Donald Cook) she loves, that her duty is to remain with Royale because of his infirmity. Realizing Grace is ready to sacrifice her happiness for him, Royal confronts her and asks that she break their engagement.

Having made this gesture, he then donates a pipe organ to a needy church and he invites Mildred, who has always loved him, to attend the dedication ceremony. Moved by the occasion, Royale volunteers to play a hymn on the new organ that he cannot hear but can spiritually feel.

What the critics said about
THE MAN WHO PLAYED GOD

Mordaunt Hall in *The New York Times:*

Besides Mr. Arliss' masterful acting, there is an excellent performance by Violet Heming, who appears as Royale's sincere and sympathetic friend. Bette Davis, who plays Grace, often speaks too rapidly for the microphone.

Rush in *Weekly Variety:*

A splendid production. . . . Bette Davis, the ingenue, is a vision of wide-eyed blonde beauty.

NOTE: George Arliss also starred in the 1922 silent version of *The Man Who Played God*. The third version, *Sincerely Yours*, produced in 1955 by Warner Brothers, starred Liberace.

With George Arliss

SO BIG

A Warner Brothers Picture (1932)

Cast Barbara Stanwyck, George Brent, Dickie Moore, Bette Davis, Guy Kibbee, Mae Madison, Hardie Albright, Robert Warwick, Arthur Stone, Earl Foxe, Alan Hale, Dorothy Peterson, Dawn O'Day (Anne Shirley), Dick Winslow, Elizabeth Patterson, Rita LeRoy, Blanche Friderici, Lionel Bellmore.

Credits Produced by Jack L. Warner. Directed by William A. Wellman. Screen play by J. Grubb Alexander and Robert Lord. Based on the novel by Edna Ferber. Photographed by Sid Hickox. Musical score by W. Franke Harling. Costumes by Orry-Kelly. Edited by William Holmes. Running time, 82 minutes.

Synopsis Selina Peake (Dawn O'Day) lived a luxurious childhood with her widowed father, Simeon (Robert Warwick), a professional gambler, who instilled in her a lifelong appreciation for all creations, natural and artistic. After Simeon died and his Chicago mansion had been sold to pay his debts, Selina's aunts enrolled her in a boarding school and forgot about her. The girl compensated for her loneliness by living for the time when she could fulfill her ambition to be a teacher in the northwest farm country.

While teaching school and boarding in the home of Klaus Poole (Alan Hale), Selina (Barbara Stanwyck), now an attractive young woman, meets Pervus Dejong (Earl Foxe), a Dutch farmer with a thirst for knowledge whom she tutors privately. Recognizing the same qualities in him that motivated her father, she accepts his proposal and they are married. Later, after their son Dirk (Dickie Moore) is born, Pervus dies, but Selina remains a farmer, believing it best to raise Dirk close to the beauties of nature. Her hopes are for him to become an architect.

With Hardie Albright

With Hardie Albright, Barbara Stanwyck, and George Brent

Selina's disappointment in the adult Dirk (Hardie Albright) is profound after he resigns an apprentice job with an architect and takes a position as a bonds salesman in a brokerage house. This has been arranged by his employer's wife (Rita LeRoy), with whom he is infatuated. Her disillusionment is intensified by her admiration of Klaus Poole's son, Roelfe (George Brent), who has become a famous sculptor.

Returning from Europe, Roelfe visits Selina and tells her that her high ideals and nobility were always his inspiration and incentive to keep going when things appeared hopeless. In Roelfe, Selina sees the fulfillment of the dreams she had for Dirk.

Coming home to see Roelfe, Dirk brings along Dallas O'Mara (Bette Davis), a young artist in love with him, who, after meeting Selina, understands the philosophy that has guided her life. Selina's last hope for Dirk's salvation is that Dallas may now be the inspiration to him that she was not.

So Big was the first of Bette Davis' apprentice films after her success in *The Man Who Played God* led Warners to sign her to a contract.

What the critics said about
SO BIG

A. D. S. in *The New York Times:*

Barbara Stanwyck is stumbling down the weary, weather-beaten years of Selina Peake's life in a new version of *So Big.* . . . The film similarly is a faithful and methodical treatment of Miss Ferber's novel, but without fire or drama or the vitality of the original. . . . Bette Davis, as a young artist who sees into the complicated story of Selina's life, is unusually competent.

In *Motion Picture Herald:*

A fine production in cast, photography, background, and direction. William Wellman has carried the episodic story along with a smoothness and sincere virility which sustained interest even when the action is slow.

NOTE: First National originally made a silent *So Big* in 1925 with Colleen Moore as Selina and Phyllis Haver as Dallas. In 1953 Warners made a third version with Jane Wyman and Nancy Olson as Selina and Dallas, respectively.

THE RICH ARE ALWAYS WITH US

A First National Picture Released by Warner Brothers (1932)

Cast Ruth Chatterton, George Brent, Adrienne Dore, Bette Davis, John Miljan, Mae Madison, John Wray, Robert Warwick, Virginia Hammond, Walter Walker, Eula Gray, Edith Allen, Ethel Kenyon, Ruth Lee, Berton Churchill.

Credits Produced by Samuel Bischoff. Directed by Alfred E. Green. Screen play by Austin Parker. Based on the novel by E. Pettit. Photographed by Ernest Haller. Musical score by W. Franke Harling. Gowns by Orry-Kelly. Edited by George Marks. Running time, 73 minutes.

With George Brent

Synopsis After ten years, the marriage of Caroline Van Dyke (Ruth Chatterton) and Greg Grannard (John Miljan), thought by everyone to be ideal, is faltering. Greg, a successful broker, is a bit of a philanderer. His latest inamorata, Allison Adair (Adrienne Dore), more predatory than his usual conquests, intends to become his second wife. Realizing she is a dangerous threat to her happiness, Caroline confides to her friend Julian Tierney (George Brent), a famous newspaper correspondent, about her problem. Having found Greg and Allison in a compromising situation she intended to overlook, she changes her mind when Julian confesses he loves her.

She goes to Paris and files for a divorce and Julian follows her there. Friends abroad tell her of Greg's marriage to Allison and that they have withdrawn their accounts from his firm because of it. Wondering if she should help Greg, who is in financial trouble, Caroline's concern for her ex-husband alienates Julian, who returns to New York.

With George Brent, Ruth Chatterton, and John Miljan

With George Brent, Virginia Hammond,
Ruth Chatterton, and Walter Walker

Caroline comes home on the next boat, but Julian is not at the pier to meet her. At his apartment she is given a cool reception and she learns he is seeing a great deal of Malbro (Bette Davis), a flashy flapper who makes no attempt to hide her infatuation for Julian. Asking Julian for a meeting at which she hopes to convince him of her love, she is prevented from keeping her rendezvous when Greg shows up unexpectedly to discuss a business matter. Indignant, Julian refuses to accept any explanation.

Later, after Allison is killed in an automobile accident in which Greg is seriously injured, Caroline rushes to his bedside and learns he has only a slight chance of surviving. She remains until he regains consciousness, promising to stay with him through his convalescence and help him re-establish his business.

Knowing that her intentions are unselfish, Julian tells Caroline he has stopped seeing Malbro. He again asks her to marry him before he leaves for China, where he has been assigned to write a series of articles. She agrees to an immediate wedding when Julian says he is willing to postpone their Oriental honeymoon until Greg is fully recovered.

Years after making *The Rich Are Always With Us*, Bette Davis wrote that Ruth Chatterton had been kind and very helpful. Miss Chatterton married George Brent, but they were divorced several years later. Rumors that Miss Davis and Brent might be in love persisted during the next eight years, during which they starred together in nine more films.

What one critic said about

THE RICH ARE ALWAYS WITH US

Mordaunt Hall in *The New York Times*:

A zealous attempt at high comedy which unfortunately savors more of Hollywood than it does of fashionable New York society, with which it is supposed to be concerned. It results, however, in being mildly diverting, owing to Miss Chatterton's charming performance and the competent acting of the others. . . . Bette Davis also serves this film well.

With George Brent

THE DARK HORSE

A First National Picture Released by Warner Brothers (1932)

Cast Warren William, Guy Kibbee, Bette Davis, Frank McHugh, Vivienne Osborne, Sam Hardy, Robert Warwick, Harry Holman, Charles Sellon, Robert Emmett O'Connor, Berton Churchill.

Credits Associate Producer, Samuel Bischoff. Directed by Alfred E. Green. Screen play by Joseph Jackson and Wilson Mizner. Based on an original story by Melville Grossman, Joseph Jackson, and Courtenay Terrett. Photographed by Sol Polito. Art direction by Jack Okey. Edited by George Marks. Running time, 75 minutes.

Synopsis A deadlock at the Progressive Party's gubernatorial convention results in the nomination of Zachary Hicks (Guy Kibbee), a dark horse contender "so dumb that every time he opens his mouth he subtracts from the total sum of human knowledge." Aware that Hicks, left to his own devices, can destroy the Party's chance of victory, his supporters agree that a specialized campaign manager is a necessity.

Kay Russell (Bette Davis), a loyal Progressive worker, suggests they hire Hal Blake (Warren William) for the job. A veteran of political wars, Blake has been adroit at helping unsuitable candidates win elections. The councilmen are enthusiastic until they hear Blake is in jail because he is behind in his alimony payments to Maybelle. his ex-wife (Vivienne Osborne). In love with Blake, Kay persuades the committee to see him after she reminds them that many great men—Mark Twain, Oscar Wilde, Columbus, et al.—spent time in prison. Overhearing Blake delivering a speech about human rights to his cellmates, the council is so impressed that they pay his fine and the alimony money he owes and prevail upon him to start to work at once.

With Vivienne Osborne and Warren William

With Warren William and Frank McHugh (left and right)

Considering Hicks to be a hopeless candidate, Blake decides that his public image should be the simple and honest façade. He revamps a Lincoln speech for Hicks to deliver on the campaign's opening night program. The opposition candidate, the first to speak, delivers the same speech Hicks had intended using. Using this to his advantage, Blake denounces the candidate by accusing him of filching thoughts from a dead man's grave. Hicks, relieved of having to make a speech, is regarded as a hero.

His state tour is so effective the opposition party starts a smear campaign to assure his defeat. They arrange a frame-up involving him with Maybelle. To avert scandal, Blake remarries her in an airplane ceremony en route to the state capital. Kay does not approve of this maneuver. But, after Hicks wins the election and Blake tells her his remarriage is not valid, she agrees to marry him. Maybelle, learning she has been duped, reminds Blake he must continue her alimony payments.

What the critics said about

THE DARK HORSE

Mordaunt Hall in *The New York Times:*

A lively comedy of politics . . . filled with bright lines and clever incidents and never a word or an action is wasted. . . . Mr. Kibbee and Mr. William leave no stone unturned to afford merriment. Miss Davis gives a splendid performance. . . .

With Warren William

In *Photoplay:*

This grand political satire, which comes at the most opportune of moments, will give you enough chuckles to tide you over a flock of gloomy days.

CABIN IN THE COTTON

A First National Picture Released by
Warner Brothers (1932)

Cast Richard Barthelmess, Bette Davis, Dorothy Jordan, Henry B. Walthall, Berton Churchill, Walter Percival, William LeMaire, Hardie Albright, Edmund Breese, Tully Marshall, Clarence Muse, Russell Simpson, John Marston, Erville Anderson, Dorothy Peterson, Snow Flake, Harry Cording.

Credits Executive Producer, Jack L. Warner. Directed by Michael Curtiz. Screen play by Paul Green. Based on the novel by Harry Harrison Kroll. Photographed by Barney McGill. Edited by George Amy. Running time, 79 minutes.

Synopsis Marvin Blake (Richard Barthelmess), an impoverished sharecropper's son, hopes to educate himself and help his "Peckerwood" neighbors in their struggle to overcome poverty and ignorance. After his father dies, Marvin is given a night job at the general store of Lane Norwood (Berton Churchill), a wealthy planter who takes an interest in him. Norwood's daughter Madge (Bette Davis), home from school, flirts brazenly with Marvin and invites him to her homecoming party. They dance continuously and Marvin, completely smitten, tells Madge he loves her.

Norwood promotes Marvin to bookkeeper, and he soon learns that the planter has been cheating his tenants out of a fair share of the profits. But, by this time, Norwood has taken him into his home, treating him as if he were a son. The planter hopes to learn from Marvin which of the sharecroppers have been stealing cotton and plotting a rebellion.

A neighboring planter is killed after surprising a cotton thief, who is subsequently hunted down by a posse Norwood has formed and then lynched. The sharecroppers retaliate by burning Norwood's store and destroying his records, which list their overdue accounts. The rebellion becomes serious enough for Norwood to threaten to call in the state militia.

The Peckerwood workers ask Marvin to join their cause and lead a movement to force the planters into giving them a contract guaranteeing better conditions. Marvin agrees to help, provided the marauding is stopped. At a meeting of sharecroppers and planters intended to be the occasion of an equitable contract, Norwood rejects the agreement until Marvin tells him he has a duplicate set of books which can prove Norwood has been cheating his planters for years. Telling Norwood he intends to take this evidence to the governor, even if it means his own imprisonment, Marvin effects a change of heart on the planter's part.

When the meeting adjourns, Marvin is acclaimed a hero. He asks Betty Wright (Dorothy Jordan), his childhood sweetheart, if he can resume courting her. Seeing them leave together, Madge feels certain Marvin is still attracted to her and that she will see him again.

What the critics said about
CABIN IN THE COTTON

Richard Watts, Jr., in the
New York Herald Tribune:

A good and apparently quite sincere attempt at real social drama, and it is aided by the earnestness of Mr. Barthelmess' acting. . . . Miss Davis shows a surprising vivacity as the seductive rich girl.

Regina Crewe in the *New York American:*

Windy film material, but it is beautified by photographic splendor and strengthened mightily by the perennially boyish, appealing star and that flashy, luminous newcomer Bette Davis, who romps off with first honors, for hers is the most dashing and colorful role. . . . The girl is superb.

With Richard Barthelmess

With Hardie Albright (below)

With Richard Barthelmess (above)

THREE ON A MATCH

A First National Picture Released by
Warner Brothers (1932)

Cast Joan Blondell, Warren William, Ann Dvorak, Bette Davis, Grant Mitchell, Lyle Talbot, Sheila Terry, Glenda Farrell, Clara Blandick, Buster Phelps, Humphrey Bogart, John Marston, Patricia Ellis, Hale Hamilton, Frankie Darro, Dawn O'Day (Anne Shirley), Virginia Davis, Dick Brandon, Allen Jenkins, Jack LaRue, Edward Arnold.

Credits Associate Producer, Samuel Bischoff. Directed by Mervyn LeRoy. Screen play by Lucien Hubbard. Original story by Kubec Glasmon and John Bright. Photographed by Sol Polito. Art direction by Robert Haas. Edited by Ray Curtis. Running time, 63 minutes.

Synopsis After a long separation, three girls, close friends at school, meet again and bring each other up to date on their personal adventures. Mary Keaton (Joan Blondell), once a tomboy hellion, has served time in a reform school and has since become a profes-sional entertainer. Vivian Revere (Ann Dvorak), beautiful and wealthy, has married Robert Kirkwood (Warren William), a prominent attorney, and is the mother of a son she adores. Ruth Westcott (Bette Davis), serious and studious, has graduated from secretarial school and works as a stenographer.

Reminiscing, the girls light their cigarettes from a single match and laugh off the superstition that this is an unlucky omen and that the third person (Vivian) to use the match will soon die. Having re-established their friendship, the girls promise nothing will separate them again.

Vivian, restless and bored, decides to take her son on an ocean cruise, and she invites her girl friends to her shipboard bon voyage party. Mary arrives escorted by Mike Loftus (Lyle Talbot), an underworld character to whom Vivian is immediately attracted. When the party disbands, Vivian, instead of sailing, runs off with Loftus. When Kirkwood learns of this, he seeks Mary's help in locating Vivian and his son (Buster Phelps). Finding Vivian in a love nest with Loftus, he sues for divorce and wins. Kirkwood, granted custody of the boy, hires Ruth, who is strongly attached to the lad, to be his companion. And realizing he loves Mary, he asks her to marry him.

Reading of Kirkwood's second marriage, Vivian remorsefully takes to drinking and using drugs. Loftus, having lost all her money gambling and unable to pay off a large debt, attempts to blackmail Kirkwood, but his extortion plan is repelled. Seeking money and revenge,

With Joan Blondell and Warren William

With Joan Blondell and Ann Dvorak

he hires three henchmen (Humphrey Bogart, Allen Jenkins and Jack LaRue) to kidnap Vivian's son.

Attempting to thwart them, Vivian is also held captive. Knowing that when the ransom money has been paid, she and the boy will be killed, she scribbles a message in lipstick on her dressing gown and jumps from a window of the hideout. She is killed in the fall, but her bizarre message alerts the police to the hideout, and the kidnappers are apprehended befort they can hurt her son.

What the critics said about
THREE ON A MATCH

Harold Weight in *Hollywood Filmograph:*

It is hard-hitting, fast melodrama, handled with real motion picture intelligence. It is well acted and Mervyn LeRoy's direction is excellent. . . . Bette Davis was ravishing in appearance, but had very little to do.

Mordaunt Hall in *The New York Times:*

Tedious and distasteful. Even Mr. William falls short of his usual high standard of acting.

NOTE: In 1938 Warners remade *Three on a Match* and released it as *Broadway Musketeers.* The trio of girls was played by Margaret Lindsay (Dvorak), Ann Sheridan (Blondell) and Marie Wilson (Davis).

With Warren William and Joan Blondell

20,000 YEARS IN SING SING

A First National Picture Released by
Warner Brothers (1933)

Cast Spencer Tracy, Bette Davis, Arthur Byron, Lyle Talbot, Sheila Terry, Edward McNamara, Warren Hymer, Louis Calhern, Spencer Charters, Sam Godfrey, Grant Mitchell, Nella Walker, Harold Huber, William LeMaire, Arthur Hoyt, George Pat Collins.

Credits Associate Producer, Robert Lord. Directed by Michael Curtiz. Screen play by Wilson Mizner and Brown Holmes. Adaptation by Courtney Terrett and Robert Lord. Based on the book by Lewis E. Lawes. Photographed by Barney McGill. Musical score by Bernhard Kaun. Edited by George Amy. Running time, 77 minutes.

Synopsis Flashy mobster Tom Connors (Spencer Tracy) believes he is the toughest guy in the world and that his political associates will help get him a fast parole after a felony conviction causes him to be sentenced to Sing Sing. Telling his girl friend Fay (Bette Davis), who promises to visit him, not to worry, he brags that he will soon be out on parole.

In prison he makes no effort to reform or conform to regulations. After instigating a near-riot, he is sentenced to three months in solitary confinement by Warden Long (Arthur Byron), a dedicated man trying to effect prison reforms and a rehabilitation program.

After ninety days in solitary, Tom, aware by now that his influential friends have deserted his cause, joins a group of convicts planning an escape. But, when he learns the break is planned for Saturday, his unlucky day, he changes his mind A stoolpigeon reveals details of the escape plan to prison authorities and those convicts involved are either killed or recaptured.

Fay, hoping to effect Tom's parole, allows a mobster (Harold Huber) to romance her, believing he can help her. While resisting his advances, she is seriously injured

With Louis Calhern

in an automobile smash-up. Warden Long, expressing concern for her life, tells Tom of her accident and agrees to let him visit her. Paroled in his own custody, Tom, without a guard, leaves Sing Sing the following Saturday morning after giving his word of honor to return that night.

Two detectives stationed in Grand Central Station, unaware of his prison pass, follow him to Fay's apartment where Tom encounters Joe Finn (Louis Calhern), a mobster responsible for sending him to prison. A fist fight ensues and Finn gets the upper hand. Fay, fearful for Tom's life, crawls from her bed and grabs the pistol Finn dropped in the scuffle. She shoots the shyster and, as the detectives break into the room, Tom escapes through a window. Finn makes a deathbed statement claiming Tom shot him. Fay is unable to convince anyone she fired the gun.

With Arthur Byron and Spencer Tracy

Tom does not return to Sing Sing and the newspapers sensationalize the killing and take Warden Long to task for allowing him to leave prison unattended. Hearing a broadcast predicting Long's dismissal, Tom surrenders. At his trial Fay admits her guilt but she is not believed. Hoping to save her further grief, Tom confesses he really is guilty. He's convicted of first-degree murder and sentenced to death in the electric chair.

Later in their careers, Bette Davis and Spencer Tracy, both two-time Academy Award winners, often claimed they would like to make another film together but, to date, *20,000 Years in Sing Sing* is their only co-starring film.

With Spencer Tracy and Louis Calhern

What the critics said about
20,000 YEARS IN SING SING

Mordaunt Hall in *The New York Times*:

In this rapidly paced film there are some extraordinarily interesting glimpses of prison routine. . . . Spencer Tracy as the central character, Thomas Connors, gives a clever and convincing portrayal. Bette Davis does well as Fay.

In *Weekly Variety*:

Of pictures having the inside of penal institutions as their locale, this is one of the best.

NOTE: In 1940 Warners remade *20,000 Years in Sing Sing* under the title *Castle on the Hudson* with John Garfield, Ann Sheridan and Pat O'Brien in the roles originated by Tracy, Davis and Byron.

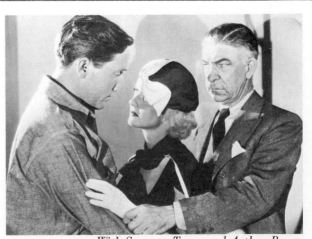

With Spencer Tracy and Arthur Byron

PARACHUTE JUMPER

A Warner Brothers Picture (1933)

Cast Douglas Fairbanks, Jr., Leo Carrillo, Bette Davis, Frank McHugh, Claire Dodd, Sheila Terry, Harold Huber, Thomas E. Jackson, George Pat Collins, Pat O'Malley, Harold Healy, Ferdinand Munley, Walter Miller.

Credits Executive Producer, Jack L. Warner. Directed by Alfred E. Green. Screen play by John Francis Larkin. Based on a story, *Some Call It Love*, by Rian James. Photographed by James Van Trees. Art direction by Jack Okey. Edited by Ray Curtis. Running time, 65 minutes.

Synopsis Bill Keller (Douglas Fairbanks, Jr.) and his buddy Toodles (Frank McHugh), once Marine flyers stationed in Nicaragua, come to New York after being discharged from service, hoping to work for an aircraft company which they discover has gone bankrupt. Wandering into Central Park, Bill meets Alabama (Bette Davis) another unemployment victim who, after hearing his story, suggests he and Toodles share her quarters to save expenses until they are back on their feet financially.

Answering an advertisement for an experienced chauffeur, Bill is hired by a Mrs. Newberry (Claire Dodd), a racketeer's mistress who finds him most attractive. Eventually he responds to her aggressive flirtations and they are caught in a compromising situation by her lover, Weber (Leo Carrillo), who changes his mind about killing him when Bill's attitude, in the face of certain death, is one of complete indifference. Impressed by this bravura, Weber hires him as a bodyguard who is to sit behind a screen in his office and shoot any visitor who threatens the racketeer. Alabama walks in one day and Weber, smitten with her Southern accent, hires her to be his secretary.

Learning from Alabama that Bill is an expert pilot, Weber uses him to fly narcotics into the U.S. from Canada and dupes him into believing he is smuggling in liquor. A government plane pursues him during a flight and Bill, thinking it belongs to hijackers, shoots it down. When he discovers he's actually been transporting narcotics, Bill threatens to quit, but Weber forces him, at gunpoint, to make another flight. During this trip they are again pursued and in the ensuing chase Bill has an opportunity to disarm Weber, dump his cargo, and land safely. He turns the mobster over to the authorities, convincing them he was forced to fly the plane against his will.

With Leo Carrillo

What the critics said about
PARACHUTE JUMPER

Mordaunt Hall in _The New York Times_:

It is a fast-moving tale of adventure in the air and on earth, and although it has some unnecessarily coarse scenes it is for the most part a racy affair. . . . Mr. Fairbanks acts with the necessary flair for his role. Bette Davis is attractive as Alabama, who speaks with a most decided Southern drawl.

In _Weekly Variety_:

Bette Davis is cute, photographically and orally, with a Southern accent that gets across. . . . A good program picture with a solid cast, sensible direction and far-above-par dialogue.

NOTE: Twenty-nine years after _Parachute Jumper_ was released, a clip from it was used in the early sequences of _What Ever Happened to Baby Jane?_ (1962), along with a clip from another 1933 Davis feature, _Ex-Lady._

With Douglas Fairbanks, Jr.

With Leo Carrillo and Douglas Fairbanks, Jr.

THE WORKING MAN

A Warner Brothers Picture (1933)

Cast George Arliss, Bette Davis, Hardie Albright, Theodore Newton, Gordon Wescott, J. Farrell MacDonald, Charles Evans, Frederick Burton, Edward Van Sloan, Pat Wing, Claire McDowell, Harold Minjir, Douglas Dumbrille.

Credits Executive Producer, Jack L. Warner. Directed by John Adolphi. Screen play by Maude T. Howell and Charles Kenyon. Based on the story *The Adopted Father* by Edgar Franklin. Photographed by Sol Polito. Art direction by Jack Okey. Gowns by Orry-Kelly. Edited by Owen Marks. Running time, 73 minutes.

Synopsis Successful shoe manufacturer John Reeves (George Arliss) is a steadfast believer in the value of advertising and takes great delight in competing with the Hartland Shoe Company because its president married the girl he loved in his youth. The Hartland Company, after the death of its owner, appears destined for bankruptcy, and Reeves, without an aggressive competitor, finds the business so dull he turns his company over to his snobbish nephew, Theodore (Hardie Albright), a conceited lad who believes he's more capable than his uncle.

While on a holiday in Maine, where he spends his time fishing, Reeves encounters Jenny and Tommy Hartland (Bette Davis and Theodore Newton), the children of his late rival. He's appalled by their recklessness: drinking; keeping late hours; and spending money foolishly. Deciding to adjust their lives, he poses as an unemployed person named Walton and establishes a friendship. Charmed by him, Jenny and Tommy offer him a factory job, which he accepts. Instead of using this rare opportunity to spy for his own company, Reeves reorganizes the Hartland factory and even fires the ineffectual manager. Enjoying a competitive challenge once again, he battles his nephew, who believes he's still in Maine, for a share of the shoe business. Impressed by his reorganization program, the bank handling the Hartland estate appoints him guardian of Tommy and Jenny.

Expecting him to be a genial puppet who will allow them to continue their profligate life, Jenny and Tommy, to their utter amazement, are told to go to work and support themselves. Tommy, put to work at the factory, learns the shoe manufacturing business and discovers he enjoys being useful. Under an assumed name, Jenny gets a secretary's job at the Reeves factory, where she hopes to learn why their shoes sell better than the Hartland products. She is also romantically attracted to Benjamin, although she regards him as a stuffed shirt.

The Hartland Company starts to flourish once more and Reeves' true identity is exposed to Tommy and Jenny, who forgive his deception and express gratitude for his help in straightening out their disorganized lives.

What the critics said about THE WORKING MAN

Mordaunt Hall in *The New York Times*:

George Arliss offers an ingratiating character study in a role that suits him well. . . . Bette Davis, whose diction is music to the ears, does good work in the role of Jenny. . . . All in all, it is a cheery but harmless little show.

In *Film Daily*:

George Arliss is most delightful and Bette Davis scores strong. There's delicious humor and the dialogue sparkles.

With Theodore Newton

With George Arliss (above) (below, left)   With Hardie Albright (below, right)

EX-LADY

A Warner Brothers Picture (1933)

Cast Bette Davis, Gene Raymond, Frank McHugh, Monroe Owsley, Claire Dodd, Kay Strozzi, Ferdinand Gottschalk, Alphonse Ethier, Bodil Rosing.

Credits Production Supervisor, Lucien Hubbard. Directed by Robert Florey. Screen play by David Boehm. Based on an original story by Edith Fitzgerald and Robert Riskin. Photographed by Tony Gaudio. Art direction by Jack Okey. Gowns by Orry-Kelly. Edited by Harold McLennon. Running time, 62 minutes.

Synopsis Advertising writer Don Peterson (Gene Raymond), in love with beautiful Helen Bauer (Bette Davis), a brilliant commercial artist, agrees to give her a chance to prove that her advanced idea of living together without benefit of clergy is an arrangement superior to marriage. Helen maintains that the emancipated woman should have complete independence in matters of the heart and that marriage kills romance. Their modern idyllic Eden works out fine until Don, about to embark upon his own business venture, convinces her they must give up her theory and get married. He contends that sin won't win him any clients.

Agreeing to be married, she argues that their marriage will only breed contempt and eventually they will hate each other. To assure her that she will never have cause to distrust him, Don asks her to take over the art department of his agency so she will be able to keep an eye on him.

With Gene Raymond

Working together, they build up a flourishing advertising agency business. In a year's time they can afford an expensive honeymoon trip to Havana. Their agency suffers the loss of several important clients while they are vacationing and upon their return they find themselves in serious financial difficulties. They blame each other for this setback.

Campaigning to rebuild business, Don focuses his attention on Peggy Smith (Kay Strozzi), a wealthy advertiser who allows Helen to believe she is having an affair with Don. Helen accuses him of being unfaithful and after an argument Don moves out of their apartment.

Helen, still in love, tries to put her relationship with Don back on their premarital status and Don is all for her idea. He claims to be enjoying complete freedom and having the time of his life. Frustrated by his attitude, Helen encourages the attentions of Nick Malvyn (Monroe Owsley), a suave competitor determined to put Don out of business.

Catching them in a compromising situation, Don now accuses Helen of unfaithfulness. Professing innocence, she confesses she only carried on a flirtation to make him jealous. Now believing his affair with Peggy was also innocent, she concedes to give their marriage another try and admits that, despite imperfections, it's a more feasible arrangement than her unconventional system.

With Gene Raymond, Bodil Rosing, and Alphonse Ethier

What the critics said about
EX-LADY

A. D. S. in *The New York Times:*

Bette Davis, a young actress who has shown intelligence in the roles assigned to her in films, has had the misfortune to be cast in the principal role of *Ex-Lady*. What that somewhat sinister event meant to her employers was that Miss Davis, having shown herself to be possessed of the proper talent and pictorial allure, now became a star in her own right. What it meant to her embarrassed admirers at the Strand on Thursday night was that Miss Davis had to spend an uncomfortable amount of her time *en déshabillé* in boudoir scenes, engaged in repartee and in behavior which were sometimes timidly suggestive, then depressively naïve and mostly downright foolish.

In *Film Daily:*

Another exposition of so-called modern views on the subject of love and marriage, with Bette Davis as the girl who wants her amorous indulgence without benefit of parson. . . . Some fairly hot scenes are sprinkled here and there but the story in general has no guts and the arguments for love without marriage are never very convincing or as shocking as intended.

With Monroe Owsley

BUREAU OF MISSING PERSONS

A First National Picture Released by
Warner Brothers (1933)

Cast Bette Davis, Lewis Stone, Pat O'Brien, Glenda
Farrell, Allen Jenkins, Ruth Donnelly, Hugh Her-
bert, Alan Dinehart, Marjorie Gateson, Tad Alexander,
Noel Francis, Wallis Clark, Adrian Morris, Clay Clement,
Henry Kolker, Harry Beresford, George Chandler.

Credits Produced by Henry Blanke. Directed by Roy
Del Ruth. Screen play by Robert Presnell.
Based on the book *Missing Men* by John H. Ayers and
Carol Bird. Photographed by Barney McGill. Art direc-
tion by Robert Haas. Edited by James Gibbon. Running
time, 75 minutes.

Synopsis Most missing persons cases brought to the
Bureau's attention are routine police work
but some requiring special attention are turned over to
the chief, Captain Webb (Louis Stone) who believes that
police resources, deductive reasoning and patience will
usually resolve every dilemma. His assistant, Butch Saunders (Pat O'Brien), is a thick-headed detective transferred from the strong-arm squad because he has been
excessively brutal. Saunders considers it working in "the
kindergarten of the Police Department." His discontent-
ment suffers the additional harassment of having Belle
(Glenda Farrell), his ex-wife, show up periodically at his
office to collect her alimony payments and make caustic
comments about his new job.

One day Saunders meets a young woman (Bette Davis)
who has applied for help in locating her husband,
Therme Roberts, missing for several weeks. Completely
taken in by her story, he makes a date with her and
promises to look into her case personally. After Webb
reads his report on the girl's case, Saunders learns her
name is Norma Phillips and she is wanted by the Chicago police for the murder of the man she claims is her
husband. Webb orders Saunders to keep his appointment
with her and bring her in.

With Pat O'Brien

With Pat O'Brien

Norma meets Saunders but when he questions her about the Chicago murder, she becomes suspicious and escapes. Threatened with demotion, he's given forty-eight hours to find her. Borrowing an unclaimed corpse from the morgue, he publicizes a story to the effect that Norma is dead and arrangements have been made for her funeral. The ruse works.

Curious to see who is being buried in her name, Norma comes to the mortuary. Saunders, waiting to arrest her, also finds that Therme Roberts (Alan Dinehart), the man she as accused of murdering, is also one of the mourners. Roberts' sudden appearance and his admission that he's the dead man's twin brother are enough clues for Saunders to piece the puzzle together. By producing the actual killer and proving her innocence, Saunders wins Norma's gratitude and appreciation. He's also forced to admit to Webb that the Bureau's work is not so easy after all.

What the critics said about
BUREAU OF MISSING PERSONS

Mordaunt Hall in *The New York Times:*

Savors of the slapstick genre of comedy. . . . Bette Davis does well and Pat O'Brien acts with necessary vigor and humor. . . . The film, for the most part, is set forth in jesting guise.

In *Motion Picture Herald:*

The picture moves fast. The dialogue is peppy and there is plenty of exciting action that leads to two surprising climaxes . . . a novel and colorful comedy.

FASHIONS OF 1934

A First National Picture Released by
Warner Brothers (1934)

Cast William Powell, Bette Davis, Frank McHugh, Verree Teasdale, Reginald Owen, Henry O'Neill, Phillip Reed, Hugh Herbert, Gordon Westcott, Nella Walker, Dorothy Burgess, Etienne Girardot, William Burress, Spencer Charters, Jane Darwell, Arthur Treacher, Hobart Cavanaugh, Albert Conti.

Credits Produced by Henry Blanke. Directed by William Dieterle. Screen play by F. Hugh Herbert, Gene Markey, Kathryn Scola and Carl Erickson. Original story by Harry Collins and Warren Duff. Photographed by William Rees. Songs by Sammy Fain and Irving Kahal. Musical direction by Leo F. Forbstein. Dances created and staged by Busby Berkeley. Art direction by Jack Okey and Willy Pogany. Gowns by Orry-Kelly. Edited by Jack Killifer. Running time, 77 minutes.

With William Powell

With Frank McHugh and William Powell

Synopsis Debonair Sherwood Nash (William Powell) has a notorious reputation as a fashion swindler who uses theatrical methods to bootleg dress designs from famous couturiers and present them to potential buyers at cut-rate prices. The Rue de la Paix salons are forced to take extra precautions and screen clients before showing their gowns.

Because his overseas agents have all been ousted from the fashion founts, Nash himself is forced to go to Paris and steal the latest designs. His two assistants accompany him: Lynn Mason (Bette Davis), a model and fashion artist who poses as a wealthy American girl interested in a new wardrobe; and Snap (Frank McHugh), an enterprising photographer who conceals a miniature camera in the head of his cane. In Paris the trio encounter Joe Ward (Hugh Herbert), a California feather merchant who hopes to interest designers in using more plumage on their creations, and Jimmy Blake (Phillip

With William Powell

With William Powell and Hugh Herbert

Reed), a struggling songwriter. Nash also accidentally meets a former girl friend, The Duchess (Verree Teasdale), who is posing as a Russian noblewoman. When Nash knew her in the States, her name was Hoboken Mamie.

Reminding The Duchess of her past, Nash promises to remain silent if she will arrange for him and his assistants to see the latest showing of Baroque gowns. Baroque (Reginald Owen), the most famous and expensive designer in France, is engaged to marry The Duchess and he grants her request. The trio take pictures and steal designs but Baroque, whose salon is well guarded with secret vantage points, is tipped off to their game. He threatens to have them arrested.

Nash counter-threatens Baroque with a newspaper scandal about The Duchess and blackmails Baroque into dropping the charges. Overwhelmed by the Nash brass, Baroque suggests he stage a legitimate fashion extravaganza. Using Baroque designs, Joe Ward's feathers and

Jimmy's songs, he devises a show that is so successful he considers marrying Lynn and going straight.

What the critics said about
FASHIONS OF 1934

Mordaunt Hall in *The New York Times:*

The story is lively, the gowns are interesting and the Busby Berkeley spectacles with Hollywood dancing girls are impressive. Instead of a stereotyped narrative about the enchantress who becomes an overnight queen of the Broadway stage, there is in this film something original.

In *Photoplay:*

Busby Berkeley's dance creations are breathtaking. Powell, Bette Davis, Frank McHugh and Reginald Owen are letter-perfect. Packed with cleverness, spectacle, beauty, sophistication and tickling humor.

THE BIG SHAKEDOWN

A First National Picture Released by
Warner Brothers (1934)

Cast Charles Farrell, Bette Davis, Ricardo Cortez, Glenda Farrell, Allen Jenkins, Henry O'Neill, Philip Faversham, Robert Emmett O'Connor, John Wray, George Pat Collins, Adrian Morris, Dewey Robinson, Samuel S. Hinds, Matt Briggs, William B. Davidson, Earl Foxe, Frederick Burton.

Credits Produced by Samuel Bischoff. Directed by John Francis Dillon. Screen play by Niven Busch and Rian James. Original story by Sam Engels. Photographed by Sid Hickox. Edited by James Gibbon. Running time, 64 minutes.

Synopsis After the repeal of Prohibition, racketeer Nick Barnes (Ricardo Cortez), who made a fortune bootlegging, is without a business. After meeting a neighborhood druggist, Jimmy Morrell (Charles Farrel), who is also an expert chemist, Barnes gets an idea for a new racket: selling counterfeit patent medicines which Jimmy can compound for half the cost of the name-brand product. He suggests that Jimmy go in business with him and when he argues that needy people will save money, the duped druggist agrees. This new income will be sufficient too for him to marry his sweetheart, Norma Frank (Bette Davis), who has been clerking in his pharmacy.

Soon after they are married, Norma begs Jimmy to give up the racket and tells him they are expecting a baby. When Jimmy approaches Barnes about getting out of the business, he's beaten and blackjacked into submission. Fearing for Norma's life, he continues working for the racketeer. Business is so good that Barnes orders Jimmy to cut production costs and dilute his imitations to where they are medically ineffective.

The scandal created by the bogus medicines almost ruins the Sheffner Drug Company, a legitimate organization whose president (Henry O'Neill) undercovers Barnes' racket and threatens police action. He's assaulted by Barnes' henchmen and threatened with death if he talks.

Norma is rushed to the hospital for a preamture delivery and her condition is serious enough so that a heart stimulant must be used. Because the medication is bogus, the baby dies and Norma almost expires. Jimmy goes gunning for Barnes but when he arrives at the factory O'Neill is there. He shoots Barnes and the racketeer falls into a vat of acid.

Confessing his duplicity in the racket, Jimmy is exonerated by the police when they learn he was forced to work under a threat of death. He's allowed to reopen his drug store.

What the critics said about
THE BIG SHAKEDOWN

A. D. S. in *The New York Times*:

It maintains a moderate sum of interest and excitement in the face of a routine assortment of gang-film impedimenta, including Charles Farrell and a howling denouement in which the racketeer expiates his sins in a vat of acid.

In *Film Daily*:

Farfetched, overacted and unbelievable. . . . Farrell and Miss Davis are not at their best.

With Charles Farrell

With Charles Farrell

With Ricardo Cortez and Charles Farrell

49

JIMMY THE GENT

A Warner Brothers Picture (1934)

Cast James Cagney, Bette Davis, Alice White, Allen Jenkins, Arthur Hohl, Alan Dinehart, Phillip Reed, Hobart Cavanaugh, Mayo Methot, Ralf Harolde, Joseph Sawyer, Philip Faversham, Nora Lane, Howard Hickman, Jane Darwell, Joseph Crehan, Robert Warwick, Harold Entwhistle.

Credits Executive Producer, Jack L. Warner. Directed by Michael Curtiz. Screen play by Bertram Milhauser. Original story by Laird Doyle and Ray Nazarro. Photographed by Ira Morgan. Art direction by Edsdras Hartley. Edited by Tommy Richards. Running time, 66 minutes.

Synopsis Jimmy Corrigan (James Cagney), a fiery-tempered opportunist, uses any method, honest or unscrupulous, to locate the heirs to fortunes left by persons who have died intestate so he might share in the proceeds of the estate after it is probated. Joan Martin (Bette Davis), the girl he loves, is so disillusioned by his business practices she resigns from his staff and goes to work for his competitor, James J. Wallingham (Alan Dinehart), whom she believes is honest. Wallingham, however, is just as dishonest as Jimmy but he hides his deviousness behind a façade of impeccable manners and serene working conditions. Believing he is the reason Joan left, Corrigan emulates Wallingham to the zenith. He purchases new and formal clothes, redecorates his office, takes diction and speech lessons and serves afternoon tea to his staff of uncouth roughnecks. Joan is unimpressed with his superficial reformation.

To prove she's wrong in her judgment of Wallingham's virtues, Jimmy sets out to expose him in a unique way. He bribes police clerks, hospital attendants and other city employees into giving him leads, and also a telephone

With Alan Dinehart and James Cagney

With Alan Dinehart, James Cagney, and Allen Jenkins

clerk in Wallingham's office. Through this informer he learns of a woman who has died intestate, leaving a fortune in bonds and cash.

A routine investigation turns up an heir to this estate but, unfortunately, he is wanted for murder and living under an assumed name. This complication does not defeat Jimmy. He devises an imaginative scheme and turns up the real killer. Having cleared his client (Arthur Hohl), he's now able to share part of the money. He also shows Joan conclusive proof than Wallingham is a scoundrel.

Corrigan rejects Wallingham's offer of a partnership and Joan rejects his marriage proposal, returning to work for Jimmy who halfheartedly promises her he will reform.

What the critics said about
JIMMY THE GENT

Mordaunt Hall in *The New York Times*:

Jimmy Cagney's latest pictorial feature, *Jimmy the Gent*, is a swift-paced comedy in which he gives another of his vigorous, incisive portrayals. . . . No such bundle of mirth would be complete without its fair lady, and she is portrayed in this instance by Bette Davis who is attractive and capable.

In *Variety*:

Jimmy the Gent is good fun and moves at breakneck speed throughout. Plot is extremely ingenious and special plaudits belong with the scenario department. Bette Davis' unusual coiffure and smart deportment help a lot. Fans that want entertainment and don't care much about cinematic art will like this one. A must for Cagney fans.

With James Cagney

With Alan Dinehart

FOG OVER FRISCO

A First National Picture Released by
Warner Brothers (1934)

Cast Bette Davis, Donald Woods, Margaret Lindsay, Lyle Talbot, Arthur Byron, Hugh Herbert, Douglas Dumbrille, Robert Barrat, Henry O'Neill, Irving Pichel, Gordon Westcott, Charles C. Wilson, Alan Hale, William B. Davidson, Douglas Cosgrove, George Chandler, Harold Minjir, William Demarest.

Credits Production Supervisor, Robert Lord. Directed by William Dieterle. Screen play by Robert N. Lee and Eugene Solow. Based on an original story by George Dyer. Photographed by Tony Gaudio. Edited by Hal McLernon. Running time, 67 minutes.

Synopsis After reading a newspaper story that alleges her stepsister Arlene (Bette Davis) is a regular customer at an underworld night spot, society girl Val Bradford (Margaret Lindsay) feels she must defend Arlene's reputation. By explaining to Tony Stirling (Donald Woods), the reporter responsible for the story, that Arlene is merely a thoughtless youngster who is unable to realize how much damage her flighty behavior does to the family name, Tony takes Val to Jake Bello's (Irving Pichel) club where they encounter Arlene in the company of shady characters.

Equally disturbed by his stepdaughter's escapades and inclined to believe she's guilty of more than mere thrill-seeking, Everett Bradford (Arthur Byron) suspects she's also responsible for influencing her fiancé, Spencer Carleton (Lyle Talbot), into jeopardizing his career by having induced him into selling stolen securities through the Bradford brokerage firm. Carleton, unable to deny Arlene anything, pleads with her to break her association with Bello and his gang because he is confronted with exposure and disgrace. To appease him, Arlene promises to reform.

Certain Bello will not let her out of the racket, Arlene gives Val a sealed envelope containing stolen bonds and

With Margaret Lindsay, Lyle Talbot, Irving Pichel, and Donald Woods

incriminating evidence which can expose Bello and the mastermind behind him and instructs her to turn this over to the police if anything happens to her. She then tells Bello what she has done.

Bello, considering her a liability, orders his henchmen to kill her, retrieve the stolen bonds and hide her body in the rumble seat of Val's car.

Concerned because Arlene has not returned, Val asks Tony Stirling and his sidekick, Izzy Wright (Hugh Herbert), to help trace the missing girl. Their course of investigation leads to their discovering that Spencer Carleton has been murdered. The trio are followed by Bello's henchmen and Val is kidnapped and taken to a waterfront hideout.

The gang demands Everett Bradford exchange the incriminating evidence for Val's life, but Tony sets a trap and dupes the unknown mastermind into leading the police to the hideout. After a gun battle, the gang is subdued and Val is rescued. A heretofore unsuspected member of Bradford's brokerage house is then exposed as the ringleader of the bond thieves.

What the critics said about
FOG OVER FRISCO

In *Variety*:

A veneer of theatricalism prevails throughout. . . . The story, in the way it's brought to the screen, never quite strikes a convincing note, starting out as it does on a questionable premise by seeking to establish the girl (Bette Davis) as one whose mental makeup and recklessness land her naturally into dangerous society and creating an almost avid desire to engage in criminal activities for coin she hardly appears to need. In spite of this, Miss Davis turns in a moderately good performance.

Mordaunt Hall in *The New York Times*:

What *Fog Over Frisco* lacks in the matter of credibility, it atones for partly by its breathtaking suspense and abundance of action. As the story of murder and robbery passes on the screen it scarcely gives the spectator time to think who might be the ringleader of the desperadoes. . . . Bette Davis does well . . . in this ruddy thriller.

With Lyle Talbot

OF HUMAN BONDAGE

An RKO Radio Picture (1934)

Cast Leslie Howard, Bette Davis, Frances Dee, Kay Johnson, Reginald Denny, Alan Hale, Reginald Owen, Reginald Sheffield, Desmond Roberts.

Credits Produced by Pandro S. Berman. Directed by John Cromwell. Screen play by Lester Cohen. Based on the novel by W. Somerset Maugham. Photographed by Henry W. Gerrard. Musical score and direction by Max Steiner. Art direction by Van Nest Polglase and Carroll Clark. Edited by William Morgan. Running time, 83 minutes.

Synopsis After studying painting in Paris four years and realizing he will never be more than a second-rate artist, sensitive, club-footed Philip Carey (Leslie Howard), returns to England to study medicine. Older and more introspective than the other students, he has to work and study long hours to remain scholastically abreast of his class.

Through two students he meets Mildred Rogers (Bette Davis), a comely but illiterate waitress in a nearby tea-room. After a date, Philip finds he's physically attracted to her and anxious to continue their relationship. Mildred later breaks a date with him to meet a loutish salesman, Miller (Alan Hale), who has promised to marry her. Philip berates her for standing him up and she inveighs against him with a barrage of insults and says she cannot become romantically interested in a cripple.

Stricken by this rejection, Philip plunges into his studies and crams for a midterm examination he barely passes. At a party he meets an attractive woman, Nora (Kay Johnson), who confesses she writes romantic novels under a masculine pseudonym. She overtly encourages a romance, even though Philip has told her of his bitter experience with Mildred.

Returning home after his strenuous examination, Philip finds Mildred waiting for him. Broke and heartsick, she says Miller did not marry her, has deserted her because she is pregnant. Phillip arranges an apartment for her. Hearing of Mildred's return, Nora bows out of Philip's life when she learns he intends marrying Mildred after the child has been born.

At a dinner party celebrating their engagement, Mildred flirts outrageously with Griffiths (Reginald Denny), a medical student she eventually runs off with. Again rejected by the slatternly Mildred, Philip once more turns his attention to his work.

With Leslie Howard and Reginald Denny

With Leslie Howard (below)

With Leslie Howard and Reginald Denny (above)

While interning at a charity hospital he makes friends with a patient, Athelny (Reginald Owen) who invites him to his home to spend a day with him and his daughter, Sally (Frances Dee), a sensitive girl whose tenderness toward Philip is not based on pity.

Mildred returns with her baby, contritely telling Philip she is sorry for having deserted him. He takes her in but hates himself for being too weak to refuse her. Mildred feels she must offer herself physically to him as payment for his charity but because she's incapable of genuine affection he rejects her and walks out. In a fit of temper she wrecks his apartment and burns the securities he needs to pay tuition expenses.

Unable to continue school, he works as a salesman until mental depression causes him to lose the job. He is taken in and nursed back to health by the Athelnys, who advise him to have corrective surgery on his deformed foot. While recuperating, Philip has news of an inheritance which makes it possible for him to return to school.

Resuming his hospital work, he encounters Griffiths, who tells him that Mildred, suffering the last stages of locomotor ataxia, is dying in the charity ward. Before he can see her, she dies in a coma. Free of his obsession, he returns to Sally and asks her to marry him now that he is certain he is capable of returning her love.

With Leslie Howard

With Leslie Howard

With Leslie Howard

With Leslie Howard

What the critics said about
OF HUMAN BONDAGE

Mordaunt Hall in *The New York Times:*

Of Human Bondage has come through the operation of being transferred to the screen in an unexpectedly healthy fashion. John Cromwell's film version emerges as a literal, intelligent and visually attractive translation of the novel. . . . In the role of the waitress Bette Davis provides what is easily her finest performance.

Alice Green in *Film Weekly:*

A big surprise was the performance given by Bette Davis as the tawdry little waitress in *Of Human Bondage.* Few people realized that she had the ability to understand and interpret the role so successfully.

In *Life:*

Probably the best performance ever recorded on the screen by a U.S. actress.

With Leslie Howard

HOUSEWIFE

A Warner Brothers Picture (1934)

Cast Bette Davis, George Brent, Ann Dvorak, John Halliday, Ruth Donnelly, Hobart Cavanaugh, Robert Barrat, Joseph Cawthorn, Phil Regan, Willard Robertson, Ronald Cosbey, Leila Bennett, William B. Davidson, John Hale.

Credits Executive Producer, Jack L. Warner. Directed by Alfred E. Green. Screen play by Manuel Seff and Lillie Hayward. Original story by Robert Lord and Lillie Hayward. Photographed by William Rees. Music and lyrics by Mort Dixon and Allie Wrubel. Musical direction by Leo F. Forbstein. Art direction by Robert Haas. Gowns by Orry-Kelly. Edited by James Gibbon. Running time, 69 minutes.

Synopsis After seven years as a copywriter, Bill Reynolds (George Brent), encouraged by his wife Nan (Ann Dvorak), quits his job and opens an agency of his own. After six disastrous months his cash reserve is gone and he still has no accounts. His one prospective client, Paul Dupree (John Halliday), a cosmetics manufacturer, is finally sold a singing radio commercial campaign because Nan got Bill drunk enough to really loosen up and properly present his ideas.

Patricia Berkeley (Bette Davis), a successful copywriter and Bill's former sweetheart, goes to work and writes a commercial for Dupree cosmetics that is so

With John Halliday

catchy the public is soon singing it. Other manufacturers are quick to bombard Bill with offers.

Patricia encourages Bill to rekindle their romance and builds up his ego. Nan, chagrined with Bill's conceit and deceit, tries to make her husband jealous by allowing Dupree to romance her. When he remains oblivious to her stratagems, she argues that he must fire Patricia. Bill refuses and asks Nan for a divorce. When she refuses this, he becomes angry and moves to his club. The next day, after returning to pick up his clothes, Bill accidentally injures his son, Buddy (Ronald Cosbey), who must be rushed to the hospital.

Before the doctor brings word that the boy will be all right, Nan reconsiders Bill's request and agrees to a divorce. Patricia, now sure of herself, makes some derogatory remarks about Nan, and Bill comes to her defense. In so doing, he realizes he still loves Nan and admits she has been the force behind his success. When their divorce case comes up for a court hearing, he admits his mistakes and implores Nan to give him another chance. Patricia, having lost Bill again, moves out of his life.

What one critic said about

HOUSEWIFE

Frank S. Nugent in *The New York Times:*

A characteristic of a poor boxer is that he telegraphs his punches. In *Housewife* the dramatic punches are not merely telegraphed, but radioed. And the most unexpected element of the film is the bewildering regularity with which the unexpected fails to happen. . . . Mr. Brent and Miss Dvorak do as well as anyone might expect, but Miss Davis is a trifle too obvious as the siren.

With George Brent

BORDERTOWN

A Warner Brothers Picture (1935)

Cast Paul Muni, Bette Davis, Margaret Lindsay, Gavin Gordon, Arthur Stone, Robert Barrat, Soledad Jiminez, Eugene Pallette, William B. Davidson, Hobart Cavanaugh, Henry O'Neill, Vivian Tobin, Nella Walker. Oscar Apfel, Samuel S. Hinds, Chris Pin Martin, Frank Puglia, Jack Norton.

Credits Executive Producer, Jack L. Warner. Directed by Archie Mayo. Screen play by Laird Doyle and Wallace Smith. Adaptation by Robert Lord. Based on a novel by Carroll Graham. Photographed by Tony Gaudio. Musical score by Bernhard Kaun. Art direction by Jack Okey. Edited by Thomas Richards. Running time, 80 minutes.

Synopsis Johnny Ramirez (Paul Muni), a night school lawyer disbarred from legal practice, takes a bouncer's job in Charlie Roark's (Eugene Pallette) bordertown casino where he makes himself indispensable enough to be given a full partnership in record time. Roark's attractive but unstable wife, Marie (Bette Davis), shows a romantic interest in Johnny but he spurns her advances and turns his attention to Dale Elwell (Margaret Lindsay), a slumming society woman who frequents the bordertown bistros.

Wanting Johnny and jealous of his attentions to Dale, Marie kills her husband by locking him in their garage after he has passed out drunk on the seat of the car. She leaves the car motor running and Charlie's death, from carbon monoxide poisoning, is later ruled an accidental one after a coroner's inquest.

With Charlie gone, Marie appeals to Johnny and when he refuses to become involved with her, she confesses she committed murder to get him. He laughs at her. Seeing Johnny with Dale proves to be too much for her and she

With Eugene Pallette and Paul Muni

59

With Margaret Lindsay and Paul Muni

With Paul Muni

confesses to the police that she killed her husband and Johnny helped her do it. They are both arrested and brought to trial.

Things go badly for Johnny until the prosecution puts Marie on the witness stand to testify. Her months in jail have had a serious effect on her mind and she goes berserk under cross-examination. Her incoherence makes it obvious she has falsely implicated Johnny. She's led from the courtroom in a state of complete mental shock.

Johnny returns to the casino where he meets Dale, who admits she is not in love with him. When he tries to force his attentions on her, she flees and is later killed in an automobile smash-up. Remorseful and disillusioned, Johnny sells his interest in the casino and donates the money to a school for underprivileged children.

What the critics said about BORDERTOWN

Andre Sennwald in *The New York Times*:

The most interesting phase of the picture is Bette Davis' performance as a cheap and confused wife who murders her husband and then degenerates under the strain of living amid the scenes which remind her of the crime. Miss Davis plays the part with the ugly, sadistic and utterly convincing sense of reality which distinguished her fine performance in *Of Human Bondage*.

John Gammie in *Film Weekly*:

Miss Davis' interpretation of a fiery-souled, half-witted, love-crazed woman is so cleverly done that one finds oneself being convinced in spite of one's better judgment.

NOTE: Warners' 1941 film *They Drive By Night* was a partial and uncredited remake of *Bordertown* with Ida Lupino in the role originated by Miss Davis.

THE GIRL FROM TENTH AVENUE

A First National Picture Released by
Warner Brothers (1935)

Cast Bette Davis, Ian Hunter, Colin Clive, Alison Skipworth, John Eldredge, Phillip Reed, Katherine Alexander, Helen Jerome Eddy, Gordon Elliott, Adrian Rosley, Andre Cheron, Edward McWade, Mary Treen, Heinie Conklin.

Credits Production Supervisor, Robert Lord. Directed by Alfred E. Green. Screen play by Charles Kenyon. Based on a play by Hubert Henry Davies. Photographed by James Van Trees. Gowns by Orry-Kelly. Edited by Owen Marks. Running time, 69 minutes.

With Ian Hunter

Synopsis Geoffrey Sherwood (Ian Hunter), a socially prominent attorney, drowns his sorrows in alcohol after Valentine Courtland (Katherine Alexander), his fiancée, jilts him for another man. Outside the church at the time she marries John Marland (Colin Clive), he's ready to create a scene but a young woman, Miriam Brady (Bette Davis), steps from the crowd of onlookers and guides him to a nearby restaurant.

She's a sympathetic listener and after Geoffrey tells her of his problems, he invites her to join him for a night on the town. When he awakens the following morning in an out-of-state hotel, he discovers he married her during his spree.

She proves to be most understanding and suggests an annulment. He insists they first give their marriage a chance. They take an apartment in Miriam's neighborhood and she becomes friendly with the landlady (Alison Skipworth), a former Floradora girl, who offers to help Miriam refine herself so that when Geoffrey's law practice starts flourishing she will be able to conduct herself properly in smart social circles.

Geoffrey soon has his practice going well and he encounters Valentine, who tells him her marriage is a mistake and she now regrets having jilted him. She tells him that if they were free, she would not hesitate to marry him. When he tells Miriam this, she offers to give him a divorce but she changes her mind after meeting Valentine in a smart restaurant. Unable to hide her feelings for her husband and ready to fight for him, she tells Valentine off in a most unladylike way. Embarrassed by her outburst, Geoffrey walks out on her and moves into his club.

Intending to divorce Miriam, he confides his plans to John Marland whom he meets at the club. Marland tells him he's a fool to forsake Miriam for a two-timer like Valentine. Suddenly aware that he really loves his wife, Geoffrey goes to see her and she welcomes him home.

What the critics said about
THE GIRL FROM TENTH AVENUE

Frank S. Nugent in _The New York Times_:

The film is credibly played by Bette Davis and Ian Hunter, and a good deal of the writing is fresh enough to make _The Girl From Tenth Avenue_ seem modestly stimulating instead of just old potatoes. . . . Miss Davis, as a growing number of filmgoers are coming to know, is one of the most competent of our younger screen actresses. Aided by a scenarist who seems to have a good working knowledge of the female brain, she gives a performance which is both truthful and amusing.

In _Variety_:

Allows the star to go high, wide and handsome on the emotions. The performance she gives should pull the picture through.

With Ian Hunter

FRONT PAGE WOMAN

A Warner Brothers Picture (1935)

Cast Bette Davis, George Brent, June Martel, Dorothy Dare, Joseph Crehan, Winifred Shaw, Roscoe Karns, Joseph King, J. Farrell MacDonald, J. Carroll Naish, Walter Walker, DeWitt Jennings, Huntley Gordon, Adrian Rosley, Georges Renevent, Grace Hale, Selmer Jackson, Gordon Wescott.

Credits Produced by Samuel Bischoff. Directed by Michael Curtiz. Screen play by Roy Chanslor, Lillie Hayward and Laird Doyle. Based on the story *Women Are Bum Newspapermen* by Richard Macauley. Photographed by Tony Gaudio. Musical score by Heinz Roemheld. Art direction by John Hughes. Edited by Terry Morse. Running time, 80 minutes.

Synopsis Curt Devlin (George Brent), ace reporter of *The Daily Express*, loves Ellen Garfield (Bette Davis), sob sister for *The Daily Star*, although he believes women make "bum newspapermen." Before marrying Curt and quitting her job, Ellen is determined to prove he's wrong.

Assigned to cover a four-alarm fire, Ellen reaches the scene too late to get through police lines but she sees two men flee the burning building and drive off in a taxicab. Sensing a scoop, she follows them but eventually loses the trail. One of the men, Marvin Q. Stone (Huntley Gordon), later dies of stab wounds in the emergency ward of a hospital and Ellen recognizes him. She scoops the other newspapers with an exclusive story.

Curt, unimpressed, tells her it was a stroke of luck, that a good reporter would track down the killer. When he hears Ellen is doing just that, he becomes interested in the case and gathers enough circumstantial evidence to have Maitland Coulter (Gordon Westcott) arrested and charged with the Stone murder. One of the people he encounters during his investigation is Inez Cordova (Winifred Shaw), a mysterious woman, who disappears.

Assisted by Toots (Roscoe Karns), a wisecracking photographer, Curt is able to eavesdrop on the jury's deliberations and accurately report the trial's progress. Ellen, anxious to find Curt's source of information, is duped into believing the "not guilty" ballots she finds in the jury's ballot box are genuine. She calls in her story to her editor, Spike Kiley (Joseph Crehan), who runs an extra issue proclaiming the acquittal. Curt's paper also runs an extra edition correctly headlining a guilty verdict.

Fired from her job, Ellen interviews Coulter at the jail on her own and believes him innocent. She also finds Curt in jail on contempt-of-court charges. Following a lead, she locates Inez Cordova and learns the truth about Stone's murder. She gets a written confession from the killer and effects Coulter's release. Her story depicting these events is so sensational Kiley gives her back her old job. And Curt is forced to admit that women too are sometimes good "newspapermen."

With Joseph Crehan

What the critics said about
FRONT PAGE WOMAN

Frank S. Nugent in *The New York Times*:

If you keep in mind that this portrayal of newspaper work is a bit on the whimsey side, then *Front Page Woman* can be recommended as a downright amusing photoplay. . . . Add to that a cast with a neat sense of comedy and you have an excellent tonic for the mid-July doldrums.

In *Film Daily*:

Given a snappy, wisecracking script, this newspaper story makes satisfying entertainment that ought to please the crowds at large. Besides the good work of Miss Davis and Brent, there is enjoyable comedy in Roscoe Karns' performance as a photographer.

SPECIAL AGENT

A Cosmopolitan Picture Distributed by
Warner Brothers (1935)

Cast Bette Davis, George Brent, Ricardo Cortez, Jack LaRue, Henry O'Neill, Robert Strange, Joseph Crehan, J. Carroll Naish, Joseph Sawyer, William B. Davidson, Robert Barrat, Paul Guilfoyle, Irving Pichel, Douglas Wood, James Flavin, Lee Phelps, Louis Natheaux, Herbert Skinner, John Alexander.

Credits Produced by Martin Mooney. Directed by William Keighley. Screen play by Laird Doyle and Abem Finkel. Based on an idea by Martin Mooney. Photographed by Sid Hickox. Musical direction by Leo F. Forbstein. Art direction by Esdras Hartley. Edited by Clarence Kouster. Running time, 76 minutes.

Synopsis Determined to end Nick Carston's (Ricardo Cortez) racketeer career and put him in prison, the U.S. Department of Internal Revenue sets out to convict him of income tax evasion. Preparing their case for a grand jury hearing, they appoint newspaperman Bill Bradford (George Brent) as a special agent assigned to gather irrefutable evidence against Carston.

Under his reporter's guise, Bill wins the confidence of Julie Gardner (Bette Davis), the bookkeeper of the Carston syndicate. He turns his charm on and she succumbs. Bill also becomes friendly with Carston, who is so congenial he gives him several tips on underworld events which help him to keep up his newspaperman's façade.

Bill reveals his mission to Julie and appeals to her patriotism to help prove Carston is cheating the government and that his syndicate has murdered several innocent people who have attempted to testify against him. She agrees to decode Carston's account books and let Bill photostat them.

This evidence leads to Carston's arrest but, confident he can beat the case, he's startled to learn from an informer (Paul Guilfoyle) working in the U.S. District Attorney's office that Bradford is a government agent and that Julie has double-crossed him. Carston orders his henchmen to kidnap Julie and prevent her from testifying before the grand jury.

Suspecting she may be in danger, Bill arranges a police guard for Julie but Carston's men manage to abduct her from the courthouse steps. Bill manages to trail them to a hideout that the police raid. Julie is rescued and brought back to testify. Indicted, Carston is convicted of income tax evasion and sentenced to thirty years on Al-

catraz Island. Because of her cooperation and testimony, no conspiracy charges are brought against Julie. Bill, in love with her, asks her to give up bookkeeping and be his bride.

With George Brent

With Ricardo Cortez and unidentified players

What the critics said about
SPECIAL AGENT

Frank S. Nugent in *The New York Times*:

The brothers Warner have turned out another of their machine-gun sagas of crime and punishment in *Special Agent*, crisp, fast-moving and thoroughly entertaining.... It all has been done before, but somehow it never seems to lose its visual excitement. . . . The Internal Revenue Bureau is personified handsomely in the reflection of contemporary manners by George Brent. Ricardo Cortez is entirely convincing as the racket lord and Bette Davis manages to fit in reasonably as the patriotic bookkeeper who double-crosses her boss for Uncle Sam and Mr. Brent (in about an 05-95 ratio).

In *Motion Picture Herald*:

Topical gangster-federal man theme, carrying the usual melodramatic, romantic contrast and only a modicum of comedy. By nature it is exciting, capitalizes on the usual suspense thread, condemning society's enemies to the "crime does not pay" tune and heroizing defenders of law and order.

DANGEROUS

A Warner Brothers Picture (1935)

Cast Bette Davis, Franchot Tone, Margaret Lindsay, Alison Skipworth, John Eldredge, Dick Foran, Walter Walker, Richard Carle, George Irving, Pierre Watkin, Douglas Wood, William B. Davidson, Frank O'Connor, Edward Keane.

Credits Produced by Harry Joe Brown. Directed by Alfred E. Green. Screen play and original story by Laird Doyle. Photographed by Ernest Haller. Musical direction by Leo F. Forbstein. Contributor to musical score, Bernhard Kaun. Gowns by Orry-Kelly. Art direction by Hugh Reticker. Edited by Tommy Richards. Running time, 78 minutes.

Synopsis Slumming architect Dan Bellows (Franchot Tone) encounters Joyce Heath (Bette Davis), a former stage star and idol of his youth, staggering along the street in the worst part of town and, wondering what misfortune has befallen her, he follows her to a speakeasy where she appears to be well known. He buys her a drink and mentions his admiration of her stage work. She tells him something of her past, alluding, somewhat mystically, to a belief that she's jinxed and a liability to everything and anyone associated with her. She confesses to being penniless and friendless.

Dan takes her to his Connecticut country home and leaves her in the care of his disapproving housekeeper (Alison Skipworth). Joyce is most belligerent and demands liquor. When Dan returns he finds her drunk. Disappointed, he suggests she try to pick up the pieces of her shattered young life.

Aware Dan is in love with her, Joyce invites his attentions, although she knows he's engaged to socialite Gail Armitage (Margaret Lindsay). He responds to her and becomes so infatuated with the fallen star that he arranges to sponsor her theatrical comeback in a play of her own choosing.

Unaware Joyce is married to Gordon Heath (John Eldredge), Dan asks his fiancée to free him so he can marry Joyce before her play opens. When he proposes, Joyce puts him off by suggesting they wait until after the play opens. Meanwhile she contacts Gordon and asks him to divorce her.

When Gordon refuses a divorce, Joyce decides to make her jinx work to her advantage. She deliberately crashes

With Franchot Tone

With Franchot Tone (above)

With Alison Skipworth (below)

her automobile into a tree, fully expecting Gordon to be killed. She escapes injury and Gordon survives too, although he will be crippled for life.

When Dan learns of the accident and the existence of Joyce's husband, he's still willing to go ahead with the play. Joyce, knowing much of her troubles have been of her own doing, suggests he return to Gail. The play opens and she is reacclaimed as a great actress. Realizing she too must make sacrifices and amends to the people she has hurt, she goes to the hospital to see Gordon, hoping he will forgive her and give her a chance to see if their marriage can be salvaged.

What the critics said about
DANGEROUS

E. Arnot Robertson in *Picture Post:*

I think Bette Davis would probably have been burned as a witch if she had lived two or three hundred years ago. She gives the curious feeling of being charged with power which can find no ordinary outlet.

Andre Sennwald in *The New York Times:*

A strikingly sensitive performance by Bette Davis in a well-made bit of post-Pinero drama. This Davis girl is rapidly becoming one of the most interesting of our screen actresses.

Grace Kingsley in the *Los Angeles Times:*

With the freshness of treatment in lines, situations and bits of business to give it reality, the tale assumes importance. . . . Bette Davis seems actual flesh and blood in *Dangerous.* That's how penetratingly alive she is and how electric, varied as to mood and real her performance in the picture.

With Franchot Tone

THE PETRIFIED FOREST

A Warner Brothers First National Picture (1936)

Cast Leslie Howard, Bette Davis, Genevieve Tobin, Dick Foran, Humphrey Bogart, Joseph Sawyer, Porter Hall, Charley Grapewin, Paul Harvey, Eddie Acuff, Adrian Morris, Nina Campana, Slim Thompson, John Alexander.

Credits Produced by Henry Blanke. Directed by Archie Mayo. Screen play by Charles Kenyon and Delmer Daves. Based on the play by Robert E. Sherwood. Photographed by Sol Polito. Musical score by Bernhard Kaun. Musical direction by Leo F. Forbstein. Costumes by Orry-Kelly. Art direction by John Hughes. Edited by Owen Marks. Running time, 75 minutes.

Synopsis Alan Squier (Leslie Howard), who considers himself an idealist by birth and a defeatist by experience, finds beauty in a service station on the barren Arizona desert where he falls in love with Gabby Maple (Bette Davis), an American-French girl with a flair for modern art and a longing to be loved. Besides Gabby, the waitress at the Maple service station, he also meets her father (Porter Hall), Gramps (Charley Grapewin), her grandfather who has a fortune in Liberty Bonds that he will not give his family, and Boze Hertzlinger (Dick Foran), a former football player with a passion for Gabby.

On the day Alan arrives at the Maple service station, Duke Mantee (Humphrey Bogart) and his gang massacre six persons in Oklahoma during a cross-country reign of terror. Gabby, already in love with Alan, persuades Mr. and Mrs. Chisholm (Genevieve Tobin and Paul Harvey), two travelers en route to California, to give him a ride.

On the road they are stopped by Mantee and his mob who steal the car and head for the Maples' station. Alan starts out on foot to warn Gabby but finds the gang in possession when he gets back.

Later, the Chisholms also come back and everyone is held at bay by Mantee. Alan, aware of Gabby's desire to get away from the desert and study art in Paris, signs over his insurance policy to her and makes a bargain with Mantee for the gangster to kill him.

A posse arrives and, after a blazing gun battle, Mantee and gang decide to make a run for it. Alan tries to stop them and Mantee shoots him. He dies in Gabby's arms, assured that she will now be able to fulfill her dream. Later, the Maples hear a broadcast announcing that Mantee and his mob have been captured.

With Leslie Howard

With Leslie Howard and Humphrey Bogart

What the critics said about
THE PETRIFIED FOREST

Frank S. Nugent in *The New York Times:*

There is a splendid character gallery in Warners' *The Petrified Forest* and it comes to life under the canny but respectful direction that Archie Mayo has given to Mr. Sherwood's play. Static scenically the picture may be, for that was the way of the play, but it is animate and vital, nevertheless, under the goad of thoughtful writing and the whiplash of melodrama that its author cracked over the back of a conversation piece. . . .

Attribute it in large part, of course, to the presence of Leslie Howard in the film edition. So well did he fit the role in the play, and so well did it fit him, that Alan Squier and *The Petrified Forest* are, by nature, inseparable. . . . And there should be a large measure of praise for Bette Davis, who demonstrates that she does not have to be hysterical to be credited with a grand portrayal; and for Humphrey Bogart, another alumnus of the play,

who can be a psychopathic gangster more like Dillinger than the outlaw himself; and, not finally, for Charley Grapewin as the garrulous old codger who sits in the Black Mesa Bar B-Q and lingers lovingly over his memories of Billy The Kid and warms his gnarled hands before the deadly flame that is Duke Mantee.

In the *Motion Picture Herald:*

The Petrified Forest is a melodramatic character drama in which the substantiating elements of romantic interest, adventure, comedy, hope and fear, triumph and tragedy and inspirational mental conflict, all held together by rigid suspense and moving to the pitch of sparkling dialogue and nerve-tensing action, are intelligently blended. It is directed and played in a manner to give the picture an aura of vivid realism, an attribute that skillfully embellishes its legitimate human interest.

NOTE: Warners remade *The Petrified Forest* in 1943 under the title *Escape in the Desert.*

THE GOLDEN ARROW

A First National Picture Released by
Warner Brothers (1936)

Cast Bette Davis, George Brent, Eugene Pallette, Dick Foran, Carol Hughes, Catherine Doucet, Craig Reynolds, Ivan Lebedoff, G. P. Huntley, Jr., Hobart Cavanaugh, Henry O'Neill, Eddie Acuff, Earl Foxe, E. E. Clive, Rafael Storm, Sara Edwards, Bess Flowers, Mary Treen, Selmer Jackson.

Credits Produced by Samuel Bischoff. Directed by Alfred E. Green. Screen play by Charles Kenyon. Based on a play by Michael Arlen. Photographed by Arthur Edeson. Musical score by W. Franke Harling and Heinz Roemheld. Musical direction by Leo F. Forbstein. Gowns by Orry-Kelly. Edited by Thomas Pratt. Running time, 68 minutes.

Synopsis The escapades of Daisy Appleby (Bette Davis), the screwball heiress to the Appleby Cosmetic fortune, are the gossip of the day and her romances are reported in headlines. The truth is, though, that Daisy is really a former cafeteria cashier who was hired by the cosmetic firm's publicity agent (Craig Reynolds) to keep the Appleby name popular.

When it is rumored that Daisy intends marrying Count Gulliano (Ivan Lebedoff), an impoverished nobleman, a New York newspaper sends its best reporter, Johnny Jones (George Brent), to Florida for an exclusive interview with her.

Hortense Burke-Meyers (Carol Hughes), the daughter of a *nouveau riche* oil tycoon (Eugene Pallette), is also interested in marrying Count Gulliano and she's so certain that Daisy is a phony that she hires a private detective to investigate her background.

When Johnny arrives to interview Daisy, she tells him she does not intend marrying any fortune hunter. Johnny suspects this to be another publicity stunt but Daisy, to convince him she's sincere, proposes that he marry her. She tells him such a marriage of convenience would be an ideal arrangement for both of them. She can continue being the social butterfly without fear of having to fight off fortune hunters and he will be wealthy enough to devote all his time to the novel he always talks of writing. Thinking he's called her bluff, he accepts. Their marriage is highly publicized and their honeymoon is a whirlwind affair of yachting, nightclubbing, polo playing and gambling.

When Johnny balks at being an overpaid escort, Daisy fears she'll lose him if he learns the truth about her. After a tiff Johnny gets drunk and is arrested for speeding. When Daisy bails him out of jail, he's paroled in her custody. Thinking she has him under her thumb while he's on probation, she insists he accompany her to all the social functions he has balked at attending. For revenge, he pays court to Hortense Burke-Meyers, who is so delighted with his attentions that she tells him Daisy is an impostor.

Hearing this, and realizing he loves Daisy as much as she loves him, Johnny kidnaps his bride and takes her to his mountain cabin where he intends remaining until his novel is finished.

With Hobart Cavanaugh and George Brent

What the critics said about
THE GOLDEN ARROW

Frank S. Nugent in *The New York Times:*

The Golden Arrow drifts rather pleasantly across the screen. It derives most of its slight strength as entertainment from the saucy performance of Miss Davis and the harried, but good-natured expression of Mr. Brent.

In *Motion Picture Herald:*

In her first motion picture since winning the Academy Award for the best performance of 1935, Bette Davis departs abruptly from the dramatic role and undertakes a straight comedy characterization heavily underscored with romance with the same brisk manner and swift utterance that has marked her other work. . . . The story is actionful and swift-moving and at no point approaches the serious.

With George Brent

SATAN MET A LADY

A Warner Brothers Picture (1936)

Cast Bette Davis, Warren William, Alison Skipworth, Arthur Treacher, Winifred Shaw, Marie Wilson, Porter Hall, Maynard Holmes, Olin Howard, Charles Wilson, Joseph King, Barbara Blane, William B. Davidson.

Credits Produced by Henry Blanke. Directed by William Dieterle. Screen play by Brown Holmes. Based on the novel *The Maltese Falcon* by Dashiell Hammett. Photographed by Arthur Edeson. Musical direction by Leo F. Forbstein. Gowns by Orry-Kelly. Edited by Max Parker. Re-edited by Warren Low. Running time, 66 minutes.

Synopsis En route by train to San Francisco, Ted Shayne (Warren William), an eccentric private detective with a reputation for being a ruthless shamus who will do anything for money, meets Valerie Purvis (Bette Davis), a shapely blonde who knows about Shayne's notoriety. She asks him to work for her and locate Madame Barabbas (Alison Skipworth), a mysterious woman she insists she must find for reasons she keeps obscure.

When Madame Barabbas learns Shayne is looking for her, she sends one of her agents (Maynard Holmes) to find out the reason. He learns nothing from Miss Murgatroyd (Marie Wilson), Shane's scatterbrained secretary, but he leaves word for Shayne to visit the Madame.

She makes him a counter-offer of a large sum of money to tell her Valerie's whereabouts so she can find out when a fabulous art treasure, a ram's horn encrusted with priceless gems, will arrive in San Francisco. Madame Barabbas tells Shayne she spent years locating this treasure and while in the Orient, Valerie, one of her agents, had stolen it and disappeared.

With unidentified player and Warren William

Suspicious of Valerie after questioning her and hearing a different story, Shayne has his partner, Ames (Porter Hall), trail her. Believing Ames is one of the Madame's henchmen, Valerie kills him. To cover her trail, she asks Shayne to pick up the ram's horn for her from her contact man who will be arriving by ship the following day.

After he picks up the treasure, Madame Barabbas and her henchmen steal it from him but Valerie also shows up at the pier and she retrieves it at gunpoint. Meanwhile, Miss Murgatroyd, fearing Shayne may be in danger, has called the police. A detective squad arrives at the pier and arrests everyone after hearing Valerie's murder confession and Shayne's bizarre story.

What one critic said about
SATAN MET A LADY
Bosley Crowther in *The New York Times:*

So disconnected and lunatic are the picture's ingredients, so irrelevant and monstrous its people, that one lives through it in a constant expectation of seeing a group of uniformed individuals appear suddenly from behind the furniture and take the entire cast into protective custody. There is no story, merely a farrago of nonsense representing a series of practical studio compromises with an unworkable script. . . .

Without taking sides in a controversy of such titanic proportions, it is no more than gallantry to observe that if Bette Davis had not effectually espoused her own cause against the Warners recently by quitting her job, the Federal Government eventually would have had to step in and do something about her. After viewing *Satan Met A Lady* all thinking people must acknowledge that a "Bette Davis Reclamation Project" (BDRP) to prevent the waste of this gifted lady's talents would not be a too-drastic addition to our various programs for the conservation of natural resources.

NOTE: *Satan Met A Lady* was a remake of a 1931 Warner film, *The Maltese Falcon,* which was made again in 1941 and directed by John Huston. The third version is still regarded as an all-time movie classic.

With Warren William

Part Two: ACCLAIM

After losing her court case against Warner Brothers and returning from England to work out her contract, Bette Davis seemed resigned to a film future that was dreary to contemplate. Certain that Warners intended to cast her only in second-rate action melodramas and indifferent program features—as a retaliatory measure, if not out of disbelief in her ability—she was pleased to be cast in *Marked Woman,* an exciting, well-written underworld story fashioned to her special talents. Two years later she won her second Academy Award, for *Jezebel,* thereby justifying rather conclusively Warners' belated confidence in her. All who doubted that her walkout had been anything but a part of the Hollywood publicity game—played to the hilt—were now aware that her rebellion was both warranted and ethical.

For the next decade, the films of Bette Davis were all of superior quality, all commercially successful and often critically acclaimed. But the public's taste in films and their support of film players, especially actresses, is notoriously fickle and follows an inexorable trend. Films change in style and pattern because of public demand and the specifications of drama and dramatis personae must be reorganized and revitalized about every seven years. After a brief period of awkward experimentation, a new wave evolves. Even adequate film actresses can usually ride the tide a couple of decades and for a third of that time they can enjoy a truly golden period. Contrary to a popular myth, actors are much more durable and movies are basically a man's medium. Intelligent enough to realize this and ambitious enough to comprehend all its ramifications, Bette Davis competed in a masculine industry with a strength ordinarily beyond her gender.

Her decline, a prospect she faced as inevitable, resulted from her inability to find suitable scripts that would add new dimensions to her already encompassing acting range and additional prestige to her already established legend. And, a mistaken belief, shared by her, her partisans, and the brothers Warner, that her mere presence in even a bad film was a guarantee of success. That belief and middle age, the equalizer of all women, co-starred in a real-life Bette Davis drama that could have been called *Comet Descending.* In Miss Davis' case, alas, the deterioration of her Warner films was not only acute, it was also unmistakably continuous. Critics who had once praised her extravagantly, were now claiming that her potency and acting economy had been replaced by all-too-familiar devices and mannerisms. And the distinctive personality that had fascinated so many had transformed itself into a caricature. In her defense, it is only fair to say that she gave too many films better than they deserved and that she never failed to meet the challenge of a superior script.

Left: (Top) With Olivia de Havilland on set of "In This Our Life." (Center) With Fay Bainter, Jack Warner. (Bottom) "The Great Lie" story conference; l. to r., Davis, director Edmund Goulding, assoc. producer Henry Blanke, George Brent, asst. director Jack Sullivan. Right: With Spencer Tracy at Academy Awards, 1938.

The films of her great acclaim period are all deserving of re-examination. A surprising number of them may collectively or individually be regarded as her best work. Into a tidy order to which I have given much thought, I cite *The Little Foxes* and *The Letter*, both directed by William Wyler, as having the best Davis performances of this period. And with them, although not quite on a par, are *The Old Maid* and *Now, Voyager*.

Stubbornly opposed to soap opera in any form, I include *The Old Maid* and *Now, Voyager*, soap operas par excellence, because they are classic examples of their film genre. Both crystallized the dilemma of women faced with the consequence of having won their emancipation and not being too certain it was a victory after all. Most of Bette Davis' films are predicated to such feminism. *The Old Maid* accomplished everything it set out to do nostalgically and tastefully. *Now, Voyager* made some trenchant social observations in an elementary but nonetheless effective way. Both films blatantly picked our sentimental pocket (to paraphrase the late James Agee) but beyond this emotional realization is a cerebral one that both are

outstanding examples of how unified a motion picture can be when all the aspects that go into its creation are intelligently and imaginatively orchestrated. Functioning as star, Miss Davis contributed exceptional performance to both films and more than likely she inspired others affiliated with them also to deliver their best.

Recently, Miss Davis discussed her long association with Jack L. Warner and said this:

"I feel very fortunate that Mr. Warner was my boss for eighteen years. He is an incredible man in that he is still the boss of Warner Brothers, some thirty-five years later. Despite our many professional disagreements, I think he ended up with great respect for me, and I hope he thanks me for those seven sound stages that I built at Warners."

The profits with which those seven sound stages were built, if Miss Davis' statement can be taken as valid—and there is little doubt that it should!—came from the films of her golden years. They comprise an admirable record, one that may never be equalled by another film actress.

With Geraldine Fitzgerald in "Dark Victory"

With Janis Wilson in "Now, Voyager"

MARKED WOMAN

A Warner Brothers First National Picture (1937)

Cast Bette Davis, Humphrey Bogart, Eduardo Ciannelli, Jane Bryan, Lola Lane, Isabel Jewell, Rosalind Marquis, Mayo Methot, Ben Welden, Henry O'Neill, Allen Jenkins, John Litel, Damian O'Flynn, Robert Strange, Raymond Hatton, William B. Davidson, Frank Faylen, Jack Norton, Kenneth Harlan.

Credits Produced by Lou Edelman. Executive Producers, Jack L. Warner and Hal B. Wallis. Directed by Lloyd Bacon. Screen play by Robert Rosson and Abem Finkel. Additional dialogue by Seton I. Miller. Photographed by George Barnes. Musical score by Bernhard Kaun and Heinz Roemheld. Musical direction by Leo F. Forbstein. Songs by Harry Warren and Al Dubin. Gowns by Orry-Kelly. Art direction by Max Parker. Edited by Jack Killifer. Running time, 96 minutes.

With Rosalind Marquis, Lola Lane, Allen Jenkins, Isabel Jewell, and Mayo Methot (upper left)
With Jack Norton and Mayo Methot (lower left)

Synopsis When racketeer Johnny Vanning (Eduardo Ciannelli) adds the Club Intime to his organization, he calls its staff together to announce the new operating policy: everyone will be required to induce customers to drink, gamble and spend freely. One of the hostesses, Mary Dwight (Bette Davis), clarifies the new setup, saying it will be a clip joint. Vanning agrees and says that anyone dissatisfied with his new policy should resign.

A few nights later Mary brings a sucker, Ralph Krawford (Damian O'Flynn) to the club. After Krawford loses a large amount of money gambling and then refuses to pay off the debt, Vanning orders his triggerman Charley Delaney (Ben Welden) to get rid of him. Krawford's murder is a grim reminder of what can happen to anyone who double-crosses Vanning or gets out of line.

David Graham (Humphrey Bogart), a special prosecutor, questions Mary in connection with Krawford's killing but she proves to be uncooperative. He orders her held without bail as a material witness. Vanning's shyster lawyer (Raymond Hatton) tells her to sit tight and "cooperate" with the district attorney. When she tells Graham she is willing to testify, he proceeds to get an indictment against Vanning. On the witness stand, however, she changes her story and Vanning is acquitted.

With Mayo Methot and unidentified player (upper right)
With Humphrey Bogart (lower right)

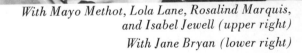

With Humphrey Bogart (upper left)
With Humphrey Bogart (lower left)

With Mayo Methot, Lola Lane, Rosalind Marquis,
and Isabel Jewell (upper right)
With Jane Bryan (lower right)

The case is well publicized and Mary's already shady reputation becomes so notorious her sister Betty (Jane Bryan) refuses to continue classes at an exclusive girls' school. She also induces Emmy Lou (Isabel Jewell), one of Mary's co-workers, to take her along for a celebration party at Vanning's penthouse. While resisting the advances of one of his stooges (William B. Davidson), Betty becomes so terrorized that the man kills her in panic. Emmy Lou, who witnesses the murder, is told to keep her mouth shut.

After hearing of Betty's death, Mary threatens Vanning by saying she intends telling the police about his rackets. Two henchmen beat her unmercifully and disfigure her face. From her hospital bed, she pleads with the hostesses to join her and testify against Vanning. When they agree, Graham offers them police protection.

The girls' testimony helps convict Vanning, who is warned not to enforce any retaliation against them or his chance of a later parole will be forfeited. Graham is acclaimed for getting Vanning convicted as Mary and the other hostesses leave the courtroom together, each uncertain of her eventual fate.

What the critics said about
MARKED WOMAN

Frank S. Nugent in *The New York Times:*

Apparently the Warners meant it when they invited the runaway Bette Davis to "come home; all is forgiven." In *Marked Woman*, which celebrates the prodigal's return, they have offered up—fortunately not for sacrifice—a dramatically concise script, a shrewd director and an extremely capable supporting cast. Not to be outdone, Miss Davis has turned in her best performance since she cut Leslie Howard to the quick in *Of Human Bondage*.

In *Variety:*

There is little doubt that, as an actress, Bette Davis has got it, and *Marked Woman* will help cement that fact. She is among the Hollywood few who can submerge themselves in a role to the point where they become the character they are playing.

Marked Woman is a strong, well-made underworld drama.

KID GALAHAD

A Warner Brothers First National Picture (1937)

Cast Edward G. Robinson, Bette Davis, Humphrey Bogart, Wayne Morris, William Haade, Jane Bryan, Harry Carey, Soledad Jiminez, Veda Ann Borg, Ben Welden, Joseph Crehan, Harlan Tucker, Frank Faylen, Joyce Compton, Horace MacMahon.

Credits Executive Producer, Hal B. Wallis. Directed by Michael Curtiz. Screen play by Seton I. Miller. Based on the novel by Francis Wallace. Photographed by Tony Gaudio. Musical score by Heinz Roemheld and Max Steiner. Musical direction by Leo F. Forbstein. Songs by M. K. Jerome and Jack Scholl. Art direction by Carl Jules Weyl. Gowns by Orry-Kelly. Edited by George Amy. Running time, 100 minutes.

Synopsis At a party hosted by promoter Nick Donati (Edward G. Robinson), prizefight champion Chuck McGraw (William Haade) harasses a bellhop, Ward Guisenberry (Wayne Morris), who knocks the champ down with one punch. The party almost ends in a brawl until Nick's mistress, Fluff Phillips (Bette Davis), intervenes and suggests to Nick that the battling bellhop, whom she nicknames Galahad, might be just the raw fighter material he can refine into a champion.

After a workout, Nick signs him for a circuit tour of second-string fights, sending his trainer, Silver Jackson (Harry Carey), and Fluff along to manage the Kid. Full of admiration and attraction for the uncorrupted fighter, whose faith in Nick is unshakeable, Fluff, against her better judgment, falls hopelessly in love with him although he remains unaware of her feelings. But she tells Nick how she feels when the tour is over and rejects his proposal of marriage. Nick belittles her until he realizes she is sincere. He mistakenly believes the Kid has cuckolded him and he intends doing something about it.

Meeting with McGraw's manager, Turkey Morgan (Humphrey Bogart), a crooked promoter, Nick arranges a championship bout between their fighters guaranteeing that the Kid will lose, but not before McGraw has an opportunity to beat him savagely.

Against Silver's objections, Nick sends the Kid to train at his farm where he becomes romantically involved with Marie (Jane Bryan), Nick's young sister.

Just before the title fight, Nick gives Ward his ring instructions, which the lad follows implicitly. He takes a savage beating and is almost defeated when Fluff and Marie prevail upon Nick to stop the fight. Suddenly aware that the Kid has never double-crossed him, Nick tells him to go in and win. After the Kid knocks out McGraw, Turkey Morgan, who has lost a fortune in bets, comes gunning for Nick. In a dressing room gun battle Turkey and Nick shoot each other.

As Nick dies in Fluff's arms, the Kid promises Marie he will give up fighting. Fluff, wishing them happiness, leaves the stadium and walks into the night.

With Jane Bryan and Wayne Morris

With Wayne Morris, Harry Carey, Jane Bryan, and Edward G. Robinson

What the critics said about
KID GALAHAD

In *Film Daily:*

Easily one of the best fight pictures ever screened. It has authenticity, suspense and romance. It was skillfully directed by Michael Curtiz and is highlighted by the performances of Edward G. Robinson, Bette Davis, Humphrey Bogart and Wayne Morris.

Frank S. Nugent in *The New York Times:*

Assisted no little by the comforting presence of Edward G. Robinson, Bette Davis and Harry Carey in his corner, young Wayne Morris, the Warners' latest astronomical discovery, comes through with a natural and easy performance in *Kid Galahad* . . . a promising debut for a new star and a good little picture as well—lively, suspenseful and positively echoing with the bone-bruising thud of right hooks to the jaw.

NOTE: *Kid Galahad* has been remade twice; in 1941 Warners remade it as *The Wagons Roll At Night,* revamping the plot to a circus background; but, in 1962, the Mirisch Brothers remade it as a prizefight musical with Elvis Presley playing Kid Galahad.

With Edward G. Robinson

THAT CERTAIN WOMAN

A Warner Brothers First National Picture (1937)

Cast Bette Davis, Henry Fonda, Ian Hunter, Anita Louise, Donald Crisp, Katherine Alexander, Mary Phillips, Minor Watson, Ben Welden, Sidney Toler, Charles Trowbridge, Norman Willis, Herbert Rawlinson, Rosalind Marquis, Frank Faylen, Willard Parker.

Credits Executive Producer, Hal B. Wallis. Directed by Edmund Goulding. Screen play by Edmund Goulding, based on his original screen play *The Trespasser*. Photographed by Ernest Haller. Musical score by Max Steiner. Musical direction by Leo F. Forbstein. Art direction by Max Parker. Gowns by Orry-Kelly. Edited by Jack Killifer. Running time, 91 minutes.

Synopsis Mary Donnell (Bette Davis), married to a gangster at sixteen and a machine-gun widow by the following St. Valentine's Day, tries to live down her notoriety by pointing her life toward a useful purpose: secretary to attorney Lloyd Rogers (Ian Hunter), an unhappily married man who loves her but keeps his distance.

When Jack Merrick (Henry Fonda), the wastrel son of one of Rogers' most influential clients (Donald Crisp), returns from Europe and professes he still loves Mary, she agrees to elope and be married that night. Merrick, Sr., traces the runaways to their honeymoon suite and insists their marriage be annulled at once. Realizing how weak Jack is, Mary gives him up although she does not stop loving him. She returns to Rogers' employ until her son is born. She implores Rogers, who learns to idolize the lad, to keep secret the fact that Jack is the child's father. Young Merrick marries again after the annulment, but his wife is hopelessly crippled in an automobile accident during their honeymoon.

Rogers, suffering from a recurrent fever, eludes his hospital attendants and comes to Mary's apartment. Before dying, he tells her he always loved her and has made

With Ian Hunter (above)

With Henry Fonda (below)

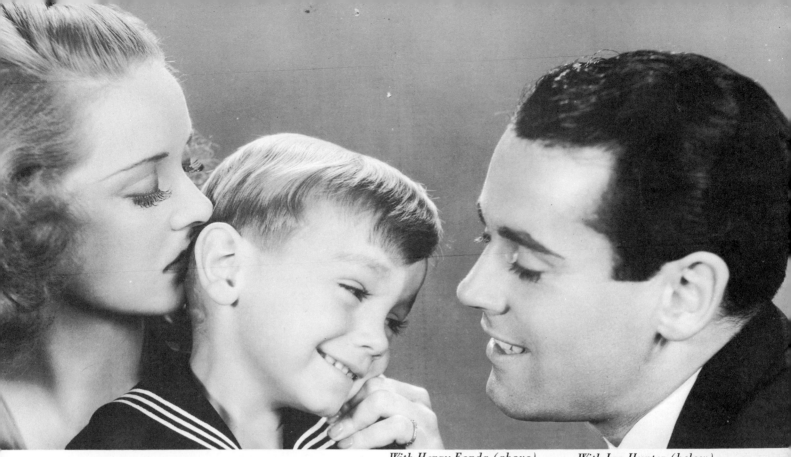

With Henry Fonda (above)   With Ian Hunter (below)

provisions for her and her son in his will. When newspapers sensationalize Rogers' death, his widow (Katherine Alexander), suspects he may have been the father of Mary's child.

Jack Merrick comes to Mary's aid and learns that the boy, now four years old, is really his own son. Merrick, Sr., hearing of his grandson's existence, institutes proceedings to have the child legally taken from its mother on the grounds that she is unfit. Rather than have that happen, Mary asks Jack and his wife Flip (Anita Louise) to adopt the boy.

She retreats to Europe and lives in seclusion on the money left to her by Rogers. After Jack's wife dies, Jack comes to see her and Mary realizes she still loves him.

What the critics said about
THAT CERTAIN WOMAN

In *Variety*:

Bette Davis shows commendable versatility in her performance in *That Certain Woman*, which demands more of her talent than any film in which she has appeared. Not a raving beauty, she nevertheless registers an abundance of feminine charm. From start to finish . . . she displays screen acting of the highest order.

Frank S. Nugent in *The New York Times*:

Miss Davis performs valiantly as usual, giving color to a role which, in lesser hands, might have been colorless as the shadows that surround it. . . . Tragic heroines (Kay Francis included) are invited to move over and

make room in their penitential niche for the Mary Donnell whose woes Miss Bette Davis manfully is shouldering in *That Certain Woman*. With the hounds of fate baying at her heels, Mary's progress through the film is pretty much of a nip-and-tuck affair, with Mary getting most of the nips. It's little wonder the Warners are calling it Miss Davis' greatest emotional role. The kind of treatment they give her would make an emotionalist out of the most stoic actress on their payroll.

NOTE: *That Certain Woman* was a remake of a 1929 film, *The Trespasser*, starring Gloria Swanson.

IT'S LOVE
I'M AFTER

A Warner Brothers First National Picture (1937)

With Leslie Howard

Cast Leslie Howard, Bette Davis, Olivia de Havilland, Patric Knowles, Eric Blore, George Barbier, Spring Byington, Bonita Granville, E. E. Clive, Veda Ann Borg, Valerie Bergere, Georgia Caine, Sarah Edwards, Lionel Belmore, Irving Bacon.

Credits Executive Producer, Hal B. Wallis. Directed by Archie Mayo. Screen play by Casey Robinson. Based on a story by Maurice Hanline. Photographed by James Van Trees. Musical direction by Leo F. Forbstein. Musical score by Heinz Roemheld. Art direction by Carl Jules Weyl. Gowns by Orry-Kelly. Edited by Owen Marks. Running time, 90 minutes.

With Olivia de Havilland and Patric Knowles

Synopsis Basil Underwood and Joyce Arden (Leslie Howard and Bette Davis), the current stage sensations, appear to be an intelligent, romantic and professionally perfect acting team. Off-stage, however, they are petty, rowdy, egotistical and fiercely jealous of each other. They have made their romance the talk of show business by postponing their marriage eleven times.

When a friend of Basil's father, Henry Grant (Patric Knowles), appeals to the actor for help in dispelling the infatuation his fiancée, Marcia West (Olivia de Havilland), has for Basil, the opportunity is too much for him to resist. He leaves Joyce in her Los Angeles hotel suite to stew while he goes off to the West home in Pasadena to spend the New Year's holiday behaving boorishly in Marcia's presence.

To shatter Marcia's hero worship, Basil insults her family, demoralizes the servants and even steals into her bedroom, making leering and flirtatious advances. Instead of being disenchanted, Marcia is so receptive Basil is forced to make a hasty retreat.

Convinced the actor loves her, she breaks her engagement to Henry. Joyce, summoned to rescue him, pretends to be Basil's estranged wife. But surreptitiously, she encourages Marcia to pursue Basil while telling Henry he has been double-crossed.

When Marcia is ready to announce her intention of marrying Basil, Joyce does rescue him by showing Marcia pictures of two youngsters she claims as her children —by Basil. Marcia rushes back to Henry, denouncing Basil as a cad. Reunited with her co-star, Joyce makes plans to get him to the altar before anything else happens.

What the critics said about
IT'S LOVE I'M AFTER

In the *New York World-Telegram:*

Must be seen! One of the most delightful and diverting comedies the madcap cinema has yet turned out.

Frank S. Nugent in *The New York Times:*

Even in a screen season which has been rich in comedies, *It's Love I'm After* must be reckoned among the gayest. It is a rippling farce, brightly written and deftly directed. . . . An agreeable change for Mr. Howard and Miss Davis and it fares extremely well at their hands.

With Leslie Howard and Olivia de Havilland

With Leslie Howard

JEZEBEL

A Warner Brothers First National Picture (1938)

Cast Bette Davis, Henry Fonda, George Brent, Donald Crisp, Fay Bainter, Margaret Lindsay, Henry O'Neill, John Litel, Gordon Oliver, Spring Byington, Margaret Early, Richard Cromwell, Theresa Harris, Janet Shaw, Irving Pichel, Eddie Anderson.

Credits Executive Producer, Hal B. Wallis. Associate Producer, Henry Blanke. Directed by William Wyler. Screen play by Clement Ripley, Abem Finkel and John Huston. Screen play contributor, Robert Bruckner. Based on the play by Owen Davis, Sr. Photographed by Ernest Haller. Art direction by Robert Haas. Musical score by Max Steiner. Musical direction by Leo F. Forbstein. Costumes by Orry-Kelly. Edited by Warren Low. Running time, 100 minutes.

Synopsis Because strong-willed Pres Dillard (Henry Fonda), the young banker she's engaged to marry, refuses to bend to her neurotic wishes, tempestuous Julie Marston (Bette Davis) intends embarrassing him publicly by wearing a red dress to the 1850 Olympus Ball instead of the customary white gown all unmarried girls wear by tradition. The ball, a highlight of the New Orleans social season, is the occasion when Julie's betrothal is to be officially announced.

Instead of creating a sensation in her scarlet dress, Julie makes a fool of herself, and Pres, feeling she needs to be taught a lesson in deportment, refuses her demand

With Fay Bainter

to be taken home by insisting she dance with him. Her humiliation is abject and she turns to Buck Cantrell (George Brent), a genial admirer who loves her, for comfort. Buck, eager to accommodate her, succumbs to her lavish compliments and escorts her home. Disgusted with her behavior, Pres breaks his engagement and goes to Philadelphia to work at a branch of his family's bank.

Embittered, but confident Pres will return and marry her when she asks his forgiveness, Julie retreats into seclusion until one day, three years later, when General Bogardus (Henry O'Neill), her guardian, brings word that Pres is returning to New Orleans, where a mild fever epidemic has short-handed the staff of his bank.

Anticipating that Pres will now marry her, she plans a homecoming party for him at Halcyon, her family estate.

Julie's euphoria is short-lived when Pres arrives at the plantation with his wife, Amy (Margaret Lindsay), whom he married while in the North. Infuriated, Julie tells Buck Cantrell that Pres insulted her and violated her honor. Buck challenges Pres to a duel but, when Pres is recalled to New Orleans where the yellow-jack epidemic is now raging, his younger brother Ted (Richard Cromwell) fights in his place, killing Buck.

The plague spreads and Pres is stricken with fever. Julie returns to New Orleans, where martial law has been enforced, to nurse him. When the militia come to evacuate him to a quarantine island, Julie begs Amy to allow her to accompany him. She promises Amy that if Pres lives, she will send him back to his wife.

What the critics said about
JEZEBEL

James Shelley Hamilton in the
National Board of Review magazine:

Jezebel is far from the usual romantic southern tale. It is a penetrating study of character in a setting whose conventional surface handsomeness does not nullify its essential truth and solidity. As in any good movie its excellences come from many sources—good plotting and writing, a director and photographer who know how to make the thing flow along with dramatic pictorial effect, and a cast that makes its story a record of living people. . . . At the center of it is Bette Davis, growing into an artistic maturity that is one of the wonders of Hollywood. The erratic and tempestuous career of this actress has saved her from playing sweet heroines and glamor girls and given her chances at parts that most players out for popularity would balk at—the result is an experience that has made her unique, in a field of character creation that is practically empty. Her Julie is the peak of her accomplishments, so far, and what is ahead is unpredictable, depending on her luck and on the wisdom of her producers.

Freda Bruce Lockhart in *Film Weekly:*

This performance is Bette's decisive victory. She handles it as though, having brought her enemies to their knees, she has decided to be merciful. By the pure power of imaginative acting she gives a performance as vivid and inspiring as any star display of personality—and an infinitely deeper level of truth. Never before has Bette so triumphantly proved her point that a woman's face can be appealing and moving even when not preserved in peach-like perfection. Never again can her claim be denied that it is possible on the screen for acting to transmute personality.

With Henry Fonda

With Margaret Lindsay and Henry Fonda

THE SISTERS

A Warner Brothers Picture (1938)

Cast Errol Flynn, Bette Davis, Anita Louise, Ian Hunter, Donald Crisp, Beulah Bondi, Jane Bryan, Alan Hale, Dick Foran, Henry Travers, Patric Knowles, Lee Patrick, Laura Hope Crews, Janet Shaw, Harry Davenport, Ruth Garland, John Warburton, Paul Harvey, Mayo Methot, Irving Bacon, Arthur Hoyt.

Credits Produced by Hal B. Wallis in association with David Lewis. Directed by Anatole Litvak. Screen play by Milton Krims. Based on the novel by Myron Brinig. Photographed by Tony Gaudio. Musical score by Max Steiner. Musical direction by Leo F. Forbstein. Art direction by Carl Jules Weyl. Costumes by Orry-Kelly. Edited by Warren Low. Running time, 95 minutes.

Synopsis At a political ball in Silver Bow, Montana, celebrating the inauguration of President Theodore Roosevelt, the most attractive girls present are the three Elliott sisters, each destined to marry a man attending the festivities.

Helen (Anita Louise), the most beautiful of the Elliott daughters, accepts a marriage proposal from Sam Johnson (Alan Hale), a middle-aged millionaire she does not love. Promising him nothing more than devotion in exchange for his love and wealth, she willingly sacrifices her youth and chance for a love match for a life of luxury. She remains loyal to Sam until he dies, at which time she is free to marry Tony Bittick (John Warburton), an Englishman who has loved her distantly for years.

The youngest sister, Grace (Jane Bryan), marries Tom Knivel (Dick Foran), the banker's son who had once been Louise's beau. They remain in Silver Bow and live a happy but prosaic life without problems other than the crisis Grace must face when Tom, in middle-age panic, has a mild flirtation with the town milliner.

Louise (Bette Davis), the eldest of the trio, follows the dictates of her heart and elopes with Frank Medlin (Errol Flynn), a handsome newspaper reporter afflicted with incurable wanderlust. After Frank deserts her in San Francisco, Louise, having just learned of her pregnancy, spends a frantic night searching for him without results. Awakened at dawn by the devastation of an earthquake, she suffers through the terror of that ordeal and is forced to vacate her almost demolished apartment when a raging fire threatens the area.

She wanders aimlessly through the devastated city in a state of shock. Befriended by a neighbor, Flora Gibbon (Lee Patrick), Louise finds refuge at the home of Flora's blowsy mother (Laura Hope Crews), where she is taken in and nursed through the ordeal of a miscarriage.

With Lee Patrick

With Donald Crisp and Errol Flynn

With Errol Flynn

Hoping Frank has survived the earthquake, she remains in San Francisco, believing he will seek her out. She takes a secretary's job at a department store operated by William Benson (Ian Hunter), a debonair bachelor who falls in love with her. While she is vacationing in Silver Bow, Frank, who has been in the Orient for three years, returns to San Francisco.

Louise remains at home long enough to accompany her sisters to a political ball celebrating the inauguration of President William Taft. Benson arrives, bringing Frank with him. Aware he has been a fool to spurn Louise's love, Frank asks her for another chance. Still hopelessly in love with him, she warmly welcomes him back.

With Errol Flynn

What the critics said about
THE SISTERS

In *Hollywood Reporter*:

Bette Davis adds still another triumph to her already long list of screen achievements. There is no doubt about the fact that she is the first lady of the screen. Her acting is a joy.

In *Variety*:

The Sisters will bring additional additional laurels to Miss Davis as a dramatic actress. As the eldest sister, she turns in one of her most scintillating performances in a superbly made production.

With Jane Bryan and Anita Louise

DARK VICTORY

A Warner Brothers First National Picture (1939)

Cast Bette Davis, George Brent, Geraldine Fitzgerald, Humphrey Bogart, Ronald Reagan, Henry Travers, Cora Witherspoon, Dorothy Peterson, Virginia Brissac, Charles Richman, Leonard Mudie, Fay Helm, Lottie Williams.

Credits Produced by Hal B. Wallis in association with David Lewis. Directed by Edmund Goulding. Screen play by Casey Robinson. Based on the play by George Emerson Brewer, Jr. and Bertram Block. Photographed by Ernest Haller. Musical score by Max Steiner. Musical direction by Leo F. Forbstein. Costumes by Orry-Kelly. Song by Edmund Goulding and Elsie Janis. Art direction by Robert Haas. Edited by William Holmes. Running time, 105 minutes.

Synopsis Beautiful Judith Traherne (Bette Davis), a fast-living member of Long Island's horsey set, appears to be the personification of youth and heiress to a rich, full life. She lives gaily but drinks and smokes a bit more than she should. The recurring headaches that plague her seem to be a social affliction but her friends are alarmed enough to arrange for her to meet a brain specialist, Dr. Frederick Steele (George Brent), at a cocktail party, knowing she would never consent to a professional examination. After an initial bit of hostility, she allows the specialist to examine her and confirm his original diagnosis: she is suffering from a brain tumor and immediate surgery is imperative.

The operation is a success and Judith falls in love with Steele, who asks her to marry him. Ann King (Geraldine Fitzgerald), her secretary, is elated with this news until Steele confides to her that Judith's brain growth will recur within a year and prove fatal. Judith accidentally learns of her true condition and after questioning Steele about her eventual doom, she concludes he only wanted to marry her out of pity. Going off the deep end, she becomes the gayest, maddest member of her cocktail crowd.

Judith's great love for her thoroughbred horse, Challenger, seems to be her only concern. One night, while in

With Geraldine Fitzgerald and Virginia Brissac

With George Brent

With Ronald Reagan

her stable talking to the animal, her Irish-tempered trainer, Michael O'Leary (Humphrey Bogart), who has been in love with her for years, overhears her. He tells her she is a fool not to grasp whatever happiness she can before it is too late. Realizing he is right, she goes to see Dr. Steele.

Once they are married, they retreat to his Connecticut farm where Steele, who has retired from general practice, intends devoting himself to research in the hope of finding a cure for brain diseases. Judith lives her idyllic summer to the fullest and each day is filled with joy and new adventure.

During the weekend that Ann King visits the farm, Steele is called to Washington for a medical conference. Judith, aware that her failing eyesight is the tipoff that she has only a few hours to live, withholds her condition from him and sends him off to keep his appointment. After he leaves, Ann helps her to her bedroom.

Lying in bed, Judith realizes she has crowded a lifetime of happiness in a few stolen months. As the last rays of sunlight disappear from her world and the darkness envelops her, she smiles, knowing she has won a small victory over death.

With George Brent

With Geraldine Fitzgerald and George Brent

What the critics said about
DARK VICTORY

Frank S. Nugent in *The New York Times*:

A completely cynical appraisal would dismiss it all as emotional flimflam, a heartless play upon tender hearts by a playwright and company well versed in the dramatic uses of going blind and improvising on Camille. But it is impossible to be cynical about it. The mood is too poig-nant, the performances too honest, the craftsmanship too expert. . . . Miss Davis is superb. More than that, she is enchanted and enchanting. Admittedly it is a great role —rangy, full-bodied, designed for a virtuosa, almost sure to invite the faint damning of "tour de force." But that must not detract from the eloquence, the tenderness, the heart-breaking sincerity with which she has played it. We do not belittle an actress to remark upon her great opportunity; what matters is that she made the utmost of it.

James Shelley Hamilton in the
***National Board of Review* magazine:**

Dark Victory is the kind of movie that will tear you to pieces if you give in to that sort of thing, and leave you wondering, after your emotions have calmed down, why you ever let yourself be moved by something so obviously aimed straight at your tear ducts. It does not take any long wondering to arrive at Bette Davis as the answer. It's her show, her special kind of show, all the way through. . . . She has never before seemed to be so entirely inside a part, with every mannerism and physical aspect of her suited to its expression. If she has deserved medals before, in parts of more dramatic validity, she deserves the prayerful gratitude of *Dark Victory*'s authors for putting life into something that must have looked pretty improbable on paper.

NOTE: In 1963 United Artists remade *Dark Victory* as *Stolen Hours* with Susan Hayward. Bette Davis received her third Academy Award nomination for her performance in *Dark Victory* and soon after its release she won her second Oscar for her *Jezebel* performance.

With Geraldine Fitzgerald

With Humphrey Bogart and Geraldine Fitzgerald

With George Brent   *With Geraldine Fitzgerald and Ronald Reagan*

With George Brent and Cora Witherspoon

With George Brent

JUAREZ

A Warner Brothers Picture (1939)

Cast Paul Muni, Bette Davis, Brian Aherne, Claude Rains, John Garfield, Donald Crisp, Joseph Calleia, Gale Sondergaard, Gilbert Roland, Henry O'Neill, Harry Davenport, Louis Calhern, Walter Kingsford, Georgia Caine, Montagu Love, John Miljan, Vladimir Sokoloff, Irving Pichel, Pedro de Cordoba, Gilbert Emory, Monte Blue, Manuel Diaz, Hugh Sothern, Mickey Kuhn.

Credits Produced by Hal B. Wallis in association with Henry Blanke. Directed by William Dieterle. Screen play by John Huston, Aeneas MacKenzie and Wolfgang Reinhardt. Based in part on a play, *Juarez and Maximilian*, by Franz Werfel and a book, *The Phantom Crown*, by Bertita Harding. Photographed by Tony Gaudio. Musical score by Erich Wolfgang Korngold. Musical direction by Leo F. Forbstein. Costumes by Orry-Kelly. Art direction by Anton Grot. Edited by Warren Low. Running time, 125 minutes.

Synopsis After Napoleon III (Claude Rains) appoints Maximilian von Habsburg (Brian Aherne), the Archduke of Austria, as Emperor of Mexico, Maximilian and his wife Carlotta (Bette Davis) land in Vera Cruz. They are met with bitter opposition from the Mexican people who are against monarchial French rule. They want the democratic government their President, Benito Juarez (Paul Muni), has been fighting to give them.

Maximilian's refusal to sign edicts which would take land from the poor farmers and return it to rich statesmen and his attempts to have the exiled Juarez appointed Secretary of State are also met with opposition from both Juarez and Napoleon. To show his strength Juarez orders a French munitions cache destroyed on the very day that Maximilian and Carlotta adopt a Mexican child as a sign of their good faith. This tyranny forces Maximilian into signing a decree which means execution for anyone committing an act of aggression against French authority. Realizing too late that it was a mistake to issue such a dictate, Maximilian finds he is merely a pawn in a political war he will surely lose because the U.S. President, Abraham Lincoln, under terms of the Monroe Doctrine, lends money and support to the Juarez cause and formally requests Napoleon to withdraw the French Army from Mexican soil.

With Brian Aherne

With Donald Crisp, Brian Aherne, and Gilbert Roland

On a mission to save her husband from certain death, Carlotta returns to France and pleads with Napoleon to help Maximilian. He refuses her demands and Carlotta, realizing she will never see her husband again, loses her mind.

Refusing to flee from the country he has come to love, Maximilian is captured and executed by free Mexican forces. Returned to the Presidency, Juarez pays tribute to the late Emperor, who he realizes was not the political puppet Napoleon intended him to be but a dedicated leader who also wanted democracy for Mexico.

What the critics said about
JUAREZ

Edwin Schallert in the *Los Angeles Times:*

This is a feature that in scope and pictorial impressiveness can well evoke the adjective magnificent. It is one of the most pretentious of films offered at any time. . . . While performances shade somewhat into the background in the panorama as a whole, there are many brilliant moments for the individual players in the picture. None perhaps more powerful than that allotted to Miss Davis when she appeals to Napoleon for aid. It is a sensational exhibition of frenzy from the acting standpoint.

James Shelley Hamilton in the *National Board of Review* magazine:

When a movie so sincere and handsome and expensive as *Juarez* comes along, done with such patent good intentions and good taste, it is disappointing not to be able to burst into involuntary and unreserved applause. . . . It is almost an ungracious thing to say, in spite of its earnest and painstaking excellencies, that *Juarez* is more of a duty than a pleasure. . . .

Most of the acting is on a superlatively high level. Paul Muni as the stolid Indian and Brian Aherne as the elegant and refined Emperor are remarkably effective contrasts in appearance, manner and speech. Bette Davis subdues her strikingly individual characteristics to a portrayal of the Empress Carlotta that is not only touching but overtoned with premonitions of her eventual tragedy, and her final flitting away into the darkness of madness is the most unforgettable moment in the picture.

With Donald Crisp, Brian Aherne, and Gilbert Roland

With Brian Aherne

With Brian Aherne

THE OLD MAID

A Warner Brothers Picture (1939)

Cast Bette Davis, Miriam Hopkins, George Brent, Donald Crisp, Jane Bryan, Louise Fazenda, James Stephenson, Jerome Cowan, William Lundigan, Rand Brooks, Cecelia Loftus, Janet Shaw, (William) DeWolf Hopper.

Credits Produced by Hal B. Wallis in association with Henry Blanke. Directed by Edmund Goulding. Screen play by Casey Robinson. Based on the play by Zöe Atkins adapted from Edith Wharton's novel. Photographed by Tony Gaudio. Musical score by Max Steiner. Musical direction by Leo F. Forbstein. Costumes by Orry-Kelly. Art direction by Robert Haas. Edited by George Amy. Running time, 95 minutes.

Synopsis After Delia Lovell (Miriam Hopkins) breaks her engagement to irresponsible Clem Spender (George Brent) and marries dependable and successful Joe Ralston (Jerome Cowan), her cousin Charlotte (Bette Davis) comforts the rejected suitor, who promises

With George Brent and Miriam Hopkins (upper left)
With Miriam Hopkins (lower left)

With Miriam Hopkins (upper right)
With Jerome Cowan and Louise Fazenda (lower right)

to marry her when he returns from fighting in the Civil War. But Clem is killed at Vicksburg and Charlotte is left to face the disgrace of unmarried motherhood. By explaining to her concerned family that she is suffering from a slight lung ailment, Dr. Lanskell (Donald Crisp), the family physician, is able to send Charlotte to Arizona to have her baby without arousing gossip.

Once the war is over, Charlotte returns to Philadelphia and starts a nursery school for war orphans. When Delia learns one of the children is Charlotte and Clem's daughter, she tells her brother-in-law, Jim Ralston (James Stephenson), that he cannot marry Charlotte because of her poor health. This malicious act causes an estrangement between the cousins which is not resolved until after Joe Ralston is killed in a riding accident and Charlotte and her daughter come to live with Delia and her children.

After Tina (Jane Bryan) grows up, she calls Delia Mother and refers to Charlotte as her old maid aunt. Because her prospect of marrying wealthy Lanning Halsey (William Lundigan) seems ill-fated because she is considered an orphan, Tina becomes bitter and resentful of Charlotte's interference in her life. Delia, hoping to bring off the marriage, prevails upon Charlotte to allow her to legally adopt the girl. Charlotte gives her consent although she plans on telling Tina the truth on the eve of her wedding. When the moment comes, however, she cannot bring herself to do it.

The following day, after Tina is married and about to depart on her honeymoon, at Delia's request she saves her last goodbye kiss for her old maid aunt. Tearfully Charlotte watches her daughter depart, knowing her only association with her in future years will come by remaining in the home of Delia, who has always resented her for loving Clem Spender.

What the critics said about
THE OLD MAID

Frank S. Nugent in *The New York Times*:

The Old Maid must be reckoned another fine theatrical property to come unimpaired to the screen. . . . Miss Davis has given a poignant and wise performance, hard and austere on the surface, yet communicating through it the deep tenderness, the hidden anguish of the heartbroken mother.

James Shelley Hamilton in the *National Board of Review* magazine:

The reproduction of the atmosphere and manners and morals of its genteel period is just about perfect, and inherent in that perfection is a quietness, even drabness, strikingly out of tune with what usually constitutes entertainment these days. The undercover bitterness between the two women in their rival motherhood is a pretty terrible thing to contemplate seriously, and there's an awful lot of suffering involved. Maybe it's just far enough away to have lost its sting, to sorrow over at a distance gently and comfortably. Maybe, though—in fact, probably—it's Bette Davis. With all her Awards she has never touched the popular heart so effectually as she has apparently done here, and that without the slightest abatement of the sincerity and histrionic integrity that is one of her strongest characteristics.

Lionel Collier in *Picturegoer*:

Once again Bette Davis has to suffer, but it's suffering in an extremely good cause, for *The Old Maid* is most decidedly going to be one of the best pictures. . . . This is one of Bette Davis' outstanding performances.

With Miriam Hopkins

THE PRIVATE LIVES OF ELIZABETH AND ESSEX

A Warner Brothers First National Picture (1939)

Cast Bette Davis, Errol Flynn, Olivia de Havilland, Donald Crisp, Vincent Price, Alan Hale, Henry Stephenson, Henry Daniell, Leo G. Carroll, Nanette Fabares (Fabray), Rosella Towne, Maris Wrixon, Ralph Forbes, Robert Warwick, John Sutton, Guy Bellis, Doris Lloyd, Forrester Harvey.

Credits Produced by Hal B. Wallis in association with Robert Lord. Directed by Michael Curtiz. Screen play by Norman Reilly Raine and Aeneas MacKenzie. Based on the play *Elizabeth the Queen* by Maxwell Anderson. Photographed in Technicolor by Sol Polito. Technicolor Director, Natalie Kalmus. Musical score by Erich Wolfgang Korngold. Musical direction by Leo F. Forbstein. Costumes by Orry-Kelly. Art direction by Anton Grot. Edited by Owen Marks. Running time, 105 minutes.

Synopsis All of England turns out to pay homage to Robert Devereaux (Errol Flynn), the Earl of Essex, on his return to London from Cadiz where he won a great victory over the Spanish fleet. In Whitehall Palace, Queen Elizabeth (Bette Davis) waits to receive her beloved. Even his detractors, jealous, power-mad advisors to the throne, are unable to overshadow his triumph. But, when Elizabeth receives Essex in her chambers, instead of congratulating him, she berates him for allowing the Spanish to sink their treasure fleet while he stormed the town of Cadiz and gathered personal glory.

Elizabeth makes her disapproval official by promoting Sir Walter Raleigh (Vincent Price), an old enemy of Essex, to a higher government post, thereby making Lord Charles Howard (Guy Bellis) the Commander of the Army and the Fleet, replacing Lord Essex. Accepting the Queen's decision and considering it a personal insult, Essex retires to his castle at Wanstead.

His friend and advisor, Francis Bacon (Donald Crisp), pleads with him to return to London, claiming that his enemies, headed by Raleigh, are plotting to have him permanently removed from the Queen's Council. Essex remains adamant in his decision until Elizabeth sends him an apology and a personal request to come to London.

In Ireland, Sir William Bagenal has just been slain and his armies defeated by the rebellious Earl of Tyrone (Alan Hale), who is leading his people in a war against English domination. When news of this defeat reaches Elizabeth, she appoints Essex as Master of the Ordnance,

With Errol Flynn

a post which will keep him from taking an expedition to Ireland to combat Tyrone. The anxious monarch fears for her lover's life.

At the council meeting Essex is duped into boasting he can defeat Tyrone and a disconsolate Elizabeth can do nothing to stop him from going.

Francis Bacon joins a conspiracy to alienate the Queen and Essex by bargaining with Lady Penelope Gray (Olivia de Havilland), the Queen's lady-in-waiting, to withhold all correspondence between the royal lovers.

Essex is defeated by Tyrone but his return to England is a cause of celebration by the people. He has visions of taking over the throne, replacing the "Tudor wench" who has ignored his pleas for men and supplies. He organizes an open revolt and seizes Whitehall Palace.

Elizabeth offers no resistance but she effects a reconciliation with her lover. Disarmed by her capitulation, Essex disbands his troops. Elizabeth then has her lover seized and imprisoned on charges of treason.

Elizabeth offers to spare his life and even to share her throne with him, but he refuses her generosity by insisting he must have complete control of England or nothing. When it is apparent she cannot bargain for his life, Elizabeth sobs as he walks from her chambers to the chopping block. In the courtyard there is the sound of drums and then a moment of silence. The executioner's axe has fallen.

With Olivia de Havilland

With Henry Stephenson and Donald Crisp

With Olivia de Havilland

What one critic said about
THE PRIVATE LIVES OF ELIZABETH AND ESSEX

Frank S. Nugent in *The New York Times:*

The Private Lives of Elizabeth and Essex (title by courtesy of Errol Flynn who felt that *Elizabeth the Queen* slighted his half of the drama) is a rather stately, rigorously posed and artistically Technicolored production which is good enough as it stands but would have been a lot straighter if Mr. Flynn could uphold his share of it.

Bette Davis' Elizabeth is a strong, resolute, glamour-skimping characterization against which Mr. Flynn's Essex has about as much chance as a beanshooter against a tank. His speeches ring with insincerity; his avowals of love are declaimed with all the conviction of a high school debater's support of the proposition that homework is ennobling. Miss Davis has hard work bringing their romantic duets off smoothly. (There were times when we felt she was afraid he was going to giggle and she overplayed her hand accordingly.) Still, the Maxwell Anderson dialogue is good to hear and the staging has been magnificent.

With Errol Flynn

ALL THIS, AND HEAVEN TOO

A Warner Brothers First National Picture (1940)

Cast Bette Davis, Charles Boyer, Jeffrey Lynn, Barbara O'Neil, Virginia Weidler, Helen Westley, Walter Hampden, Henry Daniell, Harry Davenport, George Coulouris, Montagu Love, Janet Beecher, June Lockhart, Ann Todd, Richard Nichols, Fritz Leiber, Ian Keith, Sibyl Harris, Mary Anderson, Edward Fielding, Ann Gillis, Peggy Stewart, Victor Kilian, Mrs. Gardner Crane.

Credits Produced by Hal B. Wallis in association with David Lewis. Directed by Anatole Litvak. Screen play by Casey Robinson. Based on the novel by Rachel Lyman Field. Photographed by Ernest Haller. Musical score by Max Steiner. Musical direction by Leo F. Forbstein. Costumes by Orry-Kelly. Art direction by Carl Jules Weyl. Edited by Warren Low. Running time, 140 minutes.

Synopsis Aboard a channel boat en route to France, Mademoiselle Henriette Deluzy Desportes (Bette Davis) encounters an American minister, Henry Field (Jeffrey Lynn), whom she tells about her new job as governess to the children of the Duc and Duchesse de Praslin. After landing in Cherbourg, Reverend Field wishes her luck and bids her farewell, certain they will not meet again.

Installed in the brooding de Praslin house, Henriette learns that the Duchesse (Barbara O'Neil), a voluptuous Corsican beauty, is fiercely jealous of her handsome husband (Charles Boyer). But Henriette ignores the ominous whispers of the servants and she wins the children's affection and the Duc's gratitude. The Duchesse, however, shows open resentment of her and confides to Abbé Gallard (Fritz Leiber) that she suspects Henriette is having an affair with the Duc. Abbé Gallard suggests to the Duchesse that she spend more time with her children.

One raw afternoon she insists her son Raynard (Richard Nichols) accompany her riding. The boy's slight cold develops into diphtheria and Henriette remains at his bedside, nursing him through the crisis. When he recovers, the Duchesse leaves for Corsica to visit her father (Montagu Love) but returns when gossip reaches her about the Duc and Henriette.

The Duchesse insists the young governess leave her house after enough time elapses for the scandal to fade,

With Jeffrey Lynn

With Charles Boyer and Virginia Weidler

With Richard Nichols and Ann Todd

but she does not keep her promise to supply her with an indispensable letter of recommendation. When the Duc learns of this, months later, he argues with her furiously. The following morning the Duchesse is found murdered and Henriette is arrested and suspected of being an accomplice of the Duc, who has been placed in custody in his home.

Public opinion forces King Louis Philippe to sign an order that will bring the Duc to trial. The Duc, however, takes poison. The prosecutors rush Henriette to his deathbed, hoping to hear a last-minute confession. Nothing is revealed except evidence of Henriette's innocence. She is acquitted but forced to flee the country when the enraged people of France demand Louis Philippe abdicate his throne because of his negligence in the de Praslin affair.

The scandal precedes Henriette to New York where she has taken a position as a teacher at an exclusive girls' school. Facing a classroom full of hostile students, she is forced to tell them the true story of "the notorious Mademoiselle D." When she finishes, she has won their affection. She then learns Reverend Field, who has come to visit her, arranged for her new job.

What the critics said about
ALL THIS, AND HEAVEN TOO

In *Variety*:

Anatole Litvak's direction is outstanding. Film throughout bears the mark of earnest and expert workmanship in all departments. . . . In her scenes with Boyer, Miss Davis retains an outward composure which only intensifies her real feelings, never completely expressed. It is acting so restrained that a single overdrawn passage or expression would shatter the illusion. In none of her recent films has she approached her work in *Heaven*. . . . Henriette is one of the few impressive tragic figures in modern fiction and Bette Davis gives her beauty and plausibility.

In *National Board of Review* magazine:

A long and moving adaptation of Rachel Field's popular novel. . . . Is well produced and well cast, developing its theme slowly and extracting the maximum of poignant feeling from every situation. . . . Exceptional.

With Walter Hampden and Charles Boyer

THE LETTER

A Warner Brothers First National Picture (1940)

Cast Bette Davis, Herbert Marshall, James Stephenson, Frieda Inescort, Gale Sondergaard, Bruce Lester (David Bruce), Elizabeth Earl, Cecil Kellaway, Doris Lloyd, Sen Yung, Willie Fung, Tetsu Komai, Roland Got, Otto Hahn, Pete Kotehernaro, David Newell, Ottola Nesmith, Lillian Kemple-Cooper.

Credits Produced by Hal B. Wallis in association with Robert Lord. Directed by William Wyler. Screen play by Howard Koch. Based on the play by W. Somerset Maugham. Photographed by Tony Gaudio. Musical score by Max Steiner. Musical direction by Leo F. Forbstein. Gowns by Orry-Kelly. Art direction by Carl Jules Weyl. Edited by George Amy. Running time, 95 minutes.

Synopsis One night, while her husband is away on an inspection tour of the Malayan rubber plantation he manages, Leslie Crosbie (Bette Davis) shoots and kills Geoffrey Hammond (David Newell), an intimate family friend she later claims tried to attack her.

Her account of the murder is a cool recital her husband, Robert (Herbert Marshall), believes implicitly but which is doubted by Howard Joyce (James Stephenson), an attorney called in to represent her.

While Leslie is in jail, awaiting release on bail, a messenger brings words to Joyce that Hammond's widow (Gale Sondergaard), a Eurasian woman, has possession of a letter written by Leslie in which she asks Hammond to visit her on the night he is murdered. Leslie confirms having written such a letter and confesses to Joyce that Hammond had been her lover and his death was deliberate murder.

Jeopardizing his career, Joyce agrees to help Leslie obtain the letter and pay the $10,000 for it that the Hammond widow demands. He minimizes the letter's contents and importance to Robert, who instructs him to buy it. Mrs. Hammond's only stipulation in selling the letter is that Leslie must come for it herself.

Her trial is brief and her acquittal brings cheers from the spectators. During a celebration party at the Joyce home, Robert, learning his life savings were spent to buy Leslie's letter, demands to know the contents. Confronted, she admits Hammond had been her lover and that she still loves him. Spiritually broken, Robert, still in love with her, forgives her.

Left alone, Leslie walks into the garden. An Oriental boy steps from the shadows and pinions her arms. Before she can scream, Hammond's widow appears, flashes a

With Elizabeth Earl, James Stephenson, Herbert Marshall, and Frieda Inescort

dagger and stabs her to death. As the Eurasian woman and the houseboy retreat from the garden, two policemen stop them.

What the critics said about
THE LETTER

Bosley Crowther in *The New York Times:*

A superior melodrama, compounded of excellent acting, insinuating atmosphere and unrelaxed suspense. . . . Miss Davis is a strangely cool and calculating killer who conducts herself with reserve and yet implies a deep confusion of emotions. James Stephenson is superb. . . . But the ultimate credit for as taut and insinuating a melodrama as has come along this year—a film which extenuates tension like a grim inquisitor's rack—must be given to Mr. Wyler. His hand is patent throughout.

In *Hollywood Reporter:*

One of the best pictures of the year. . . . Bette Davis has to divide honors of this great triumph with, first, William Wyler, the director, and, secondly, with Max Steiner for his most interpretive music; this triple creation was the height of fine picture-making. The star was never better in a role that called on every ounce of her great ability. Wyler's handling of his people and his direction of Tony Gaudio in the photographing, was nothing short of genius. The musical background of Max Steiner is truly his masterpiece, and a great contributing factor to the success of the show.

NOTE: In Paramount's 1929 version of *The Letter*, Herbert Marshall, the husband in the 1940 Warner version, played the murdered lover. A third version of *The Letter*, made by Warners in 1947, was titled *The Unfaithful*.

With James Stephenson (above, in foreground)

With James Stephenson (below)

THE GREAT LIE

A Warner Brothers First National Picture (1941)

With Mary Astor

Cast Bette Davis, George Brent, Mary Astor, Lucile Watson, Hattie McDaniel, Grant Mitchell, Jerome Cowan, Sam McDaniel, Thurston Hall, Russell Hicks, Charles Trowbridge, Virginia Brissac, Olin Howland, J. Farrell MacDonald, Doris Lloyd, Addison Richards, Georgia Caine, Alphonse Martell.

Credits Produced by Hal B. Wallis in association with Henry Blanke. Directed by Edmund Goulding. Screen play by Lenore Coffee. Based on the novel *January Heights* by Polan Banks. Photographed by Tony Gaudio. Musical score by Max Steiner. Musical direction by Leo F. Forbstein. Gowns by Orry-Kelly. Art direction by Carl Jules Weyl. Edited by Ralph Dawson. Running time, 102 minutes.

Synopsis A weekend of wild celebration culminates when concert pianist Sandra Kovak (Mary Astor) elopes with playboy-aviator Pete Van Allen (George Brent). They soon learn their marriage is illegal because Sandra's divorce had not been final. Pete asks

With Mary Astor and George Brent

her to marry him again the following week when she will be legally free but she insists a concert engagement in Philadelphia cannot be postponed. Relieved of his obligation, Pete flies to the Maryland plantation of his former fiancée, Maggie Patterson (Bette Davis), who broke her engagement to him because of his reckless ways.

Pete begs her forgiveness and promises to change. Confessing she still loves him, Maggie agrees to marry him at once when she hears his marriage to Sandra is invalid. Their honeymoon, however, is curtailed when Pete is called to Washington and commissioned to make a government survey flight of South American terrain.

With Pete away, Maggie goes to New York on a shopping trip and encounters Sandra, who tells her she is going to have a baby by Pete. Sandra believes that Pete, when he hears this news, will divorce Maggie and return to her. Later that day word reaches Maggie that Pete's plane crashed in the jungle.

Heartbroken, Maggie offers to make a cash settlement on Sandra if she will allow her to adopt Pete's baby. Sandra agrees and the two women retreat to a lonely Arizona ranch where the boy is born. Returning to Maryland, Maggie introduces the child as her own.

Months later, Pete, who survived the crash, comes home but Maggie refrains from telling him the truth about his son. When Sandra returns from an Australian concert tour, she visits the plantation and insists Maggie tell Pete about the baby.

He reproves Maggie for lying to him but confesses he still loves her and is willing to let Sandra have the child. When she realizes she may have the child, but not Pete, Sandra decides to leave him with his father and Maggie —the boy's real "mother."

What the critics said about
THE GREAT LIE

Bosley Crowther in *The New York Times:*

The acting is impressive, the direction of Edmund Goulding makes for class, but the story is such a trifle that it hardly seems worth the while. However, the women will probably love it, since fibs are so provocative of fun. . . . The only excuse to be found for this thoroughly synthetic tale is that it gives Miss Davis an opportunity to display her fine talent for distress, to be maternal and noble, the "good" woman opposed to the "bad."

In *Variety:*

The Great Lie is a sophisticated drama utilizing the eternal triangle formula with some new twists, providing Bette Davis with opportunity for continued display of her tragic emotionalism . . . a most persuasive portrayal.

In *Hollywood Reporter:*

As polished an offering as the combined talents of its cast, producers, director and screenplay writer can make it. . . . Miss Davis plays the second wife to erase any hint of theatricalism from the part. It is not her most spectacular performance, yet she brings it praiseworthy sincerity. In her final speech, she is generous to her rival in the story. As a star, she is even more generous to the actress who plays the part.

Mary Astor's portrayal of the concert pianist is a dazzling job. It will give this lovely artist's career tremendous impetus, send her to the top where she belongs. The fascinating character she draws is brittle, selfish, spoiled. Her playing is beautiful, and so is she.

With Mary Astor

THE BRIDE CAME C.O.D.

A Warner Brothers First National Picture (1941)

Cast James Cagney, Bette Davis, Stuart Erwin, Jack Carson, George Tobias, Eugene Pallette, Harry Davenport, William Frawley, Edward Brophy, Harry Holman, Chick Chandler, Keith Douglas, Herbert Anderson, Creighton Hale, Frank Mayo, (William) DeWolf Hopper, Jack Mower, William Newell.

Credits Produced by Hal B. Wallis in association with William Cagney. Directed by William Keighley. Screen play by Julius J. and Philip G. Epstein. Based on a story by Kenneth Earl and M. M. Musselman. Photographed by Ernest Haller. Musical score by Max Steiner. Musical direction by Leo F. Forbstein. Gowns by Orry-Kelly. Art direction by Ted Smith. Edited by Thomas Richards. Running time, 90 minutes.

With Stuart Erwin and Jack Carson (upper left)
With James Cagney (lower left)

Synopsis At the instigation of radio gossip Tommy Keenan (Stuart Erwin), Joan Winfield (Bette Davis), a headline-happy oil heiress, agrees to elope to Yuma and marry Allen Brice (Jack Carson), a Hollywood bandleader she has known four days. The runaways charter a plane owned and piloted by Steve Collins (James Cagney), a down-on-his-luck operator whose aircraft is about to be repossessed.

Learning of his daughter's plans, Lucius K. Winfield (Eugene Pallette) calls her at Collins' office and tries to talk her out of the elopement. After she hangs up on him, Steve calls him back and offers to deliver her, unmarried, to the Winfield ranch in Texas for the freight rate of $10 a pound. When told to go ahead, he gets Tommy and Allen off the plane by a ruse and flies off with Joan, who believes she is being kidnaped.

She offers him a reward to take her back to Los Angeles but he refuses, telling her that he is getting a better price from her father. Furious, she attempts to bail out but he restrains her. During their struggle the plane develops engine trouble and Steve makes a forced landing near a desert ghost town. In a runaway attempt, Joan jumps from the plane but falls into a cactus patch. After removing castus needles from her *derrière* and radioing

With James Cagney (upper right)
With James Cagney and Harry Davenport (lower right)

his location to her father, Steve drags her to the ghost town where they discover the sole inhabitant is Pop Tolliver (Harry Davenport), a desert hermit.

Believing Joan's story that Steve has kidnaped her, Pop locks him in the jail and gives Joan a room in the rundown hotel.

The following morning Allen arrives with a Nevada justice of the peace. To spite Steve, whom she realizes she loves, Joan marries Allen. Her father arrives to take her home and refuses to pay Steve the freight charges until he discovers Joan's marriage is illegal because the ceremony was performed in California, not Nevada. Telling Joan he loves her, Steve says the only reason he will consider marrying her is because her father is a millionaire.

With Harry Davenport

What the critics said about
THE BRIDE CAME C.O.D.

In *Look:*

The Bride Came C.O.D. aims at hard-hitting comedy effects and gets them. . . . Miss Davis attacks a comedy role with the same forthrightness and vigor that have characterized her dramatic assignments. She exhibits a new taste for roughhouse cinematics, and some of her comedy scenes are among the film's highlights. Cagney, of course, as an old hand, is easily her match throughout.

Theodore Strauss in *The New York Times:*

The Bride Came C.O.D. is neither the funniest comedy in history, nor the shortest distance between two points. But for the most part it is a serviceable romp. . . . As the comic sparring partner of James Cagney, no slouch himself, Miss Davis has taken the bit in her teeth and flung her breathless way through a rough-and-tumble comedy, no gags barred.

Viola Hegyi Swisher in the *Hollywood Citizen News:*

That much needed change of pace so often recommended recently for Bette Davis comes to her at last in *The Bride Came C.O.D.*, a comedy which manages to be fast or funny or both during most of the running time. . . . Max Steiner's musical score is as graphic and humorous as anything in the picture.

With Jack Carson and James Cagney

THE LITTLE FOXES

A Samuel Goldwyn Production Released by
RKO Radio Pictures, Inc. (1941)

Cast Bette Davis, Herbert Marshall, Teresa Wright, Richard Carlson, Patricia Collinge, Dan Duryea, Charles Dingle, Carl Benton Reid, Jessie Grayson, John Marriott, Russell Hicks, Lucien Littlefield, Virginia Brissac.

Credits Produced by Samuel Goldwyn. Directed by William Wyler. Screen play by Lillian Hellman, based on her stage play. Additional scenes and dialogue by Arthur Kober, Dorothy Parker and Alan Campbell. Photographed by Gregg Toland. Musical score and direction by Meredith Willson. Costumes by Orry-Kelly. Art direction by Stephen Goosson. Edited by Daniel Mandell. Running time, 115 minutes.

Synopsis Needing $75,000 to buy an interest in a sweatshop enterprise that her brothers claim will net millions, Regina Giddens (Bette Davis) sends her daughter Alexandra (Teresa Wright) to Baltimore to bring her husband Horace (Herbert Marshall) back from a sanitarium where he has been recovering from a heart attack. Arriving home, Horace is badgered by Regina but he remains firm in his refusal to give her the money necessary to finance brothers Ben (Charles Dingle) and Oscar (Carl Benton Reid) in their business venture.

When Regina is unable to inveigle the money from Horace, their nephew, Leo (Dan Duryea), an employee at his bank, steals enough negotiable bonds from Horace's strongbox to put up the necessary financing for the gin mill. Suspecting the theft, Regina tries to blackmail

With Richard Carlson

With Carl Benton Reid, Charles Dingle, and Dan Duryea

Ben and Oscar into giving her a share of the business but Horace thwarts her by claiming he gave the securities to Leo.

Infuriated because he will not expose Leo, Regina cajoles him to where he suffers a coronary seizure and must beg her for his heart stimulant. She withholds the medication from him, knowing he will die without it. Standing by his deathbed, Regina coldly defies him to make a last-minute accusation but Horace uses all his ebbing strength to comfort Alexandra and to inspire her to get away from her scheming mother and marry David Hewlitt (Richard Carlson), a young newspaper editor whom Regina has rejected as a suitor for her daughter.

After Horace dies, Regina confronts her brothers with proof of Leo's theft and demands a two-third share in their new business in exchange for her silence. They agree to her demands although Ben suggests Regina may end up being charged with murdering Horace. Defying them, she claims they have no evidence on which to base their suspicions.

Overhearing Regina, Alexandra realizes at last how vicious her mother really is. Denouncing her and saying she cannot continue living in the same house with the woman who murdered her father, Alexandra goes to David, who is waiting outside to comfort her.

From an upstairs window, Regina watches them walk off together. In possession of the power and wealth she schemed and killed to achieve, she stands completely alone, unloved and unwanted by anyone.

With Teresa Wright

With Charles Dingle and Carl Benton Reid

With Charles Dingle, Patricia Collinge, Herbert Marshall, and Carl Benton Reid

What the critics said about
THE LITTLE FOXES

Howard Barnes in the *New York Herald Tribune*:

Flawless and fascinating. . . . When a really fine film comes along it is up to all of us who really like fine films to cheer. Cheer, then, this Sabbath for *The Little Foxes*. For this adaptation of a striking play is not only a great show and an absorbing entertainment. It charts a whole new course of motion-picture making. . . . Bette Davis matches Miss Bankhead's splendid portrayal in the play.

Bosley Crowther in *The New York Times*:

The Little Foxes leaps to the front as the most bitingly sinister picture of the year and as one of the most cruelly realistic character studies yet shown on the screen. . . . Miss Davis' performance in the role which Tallulah Bankhead played so brassily on the stage is abundant with color and mood.

The Little Foxes will not increase your admiration for mankind. It is cold, cynical. But it is a very exciting picture to watch in a comfortably objective way, especially if you enjoy expert stabbing-in-the-back.

THE MAN WHO CAME TO DINNER

A Warner Brothers First National Picture (1941)

Cast Bette Davis, Ann Sheridan, Monty Woolley, Richard Travis, Jimmy Durante, Reginald Gardiner, Billie Burke, Elisabeth Fraser, Grant Mitchell, George Barbier, Mary Wickes, Russell Arms, Ruth Vivian, Edwin Stanley, Charles Drake, Nanette Vallon, John Ridgely.

Credits Produced by Hal B. Wallis in association with Jerry Wald and Jack Saper. Directed by William Keighley. Screen play by Julius J. and Philip G. Epstein. Based on the play by George S. Kaufman and Moss Hart. Photographed by Tony Gaudio. Musical score by Frederick Hollander. Musical direction by Leo F. Forbstein. Gowns by Orry-Kelly. Art direction by Robert Haas. Edited by Jack Killifer. Running time, 112 minutes.

Synopsis During a cross-country lecture tour, Sheridan Whiteside (Monty Woolley), international wit, reluctantly accepts an invitation to dine with a leading Ohio family. Arriving with Maggie Cutler (Bette Davis), his secretary, he slips on some ice outside his host's home and is carried inside shouting threats of a lawsuit.

With Monty Woolley and Ann Sheridan

Cowed by his threats, Ernest Stanley (Grant Mitchell), who is the antithesis of all Whiteside believes in, and his social-climbing wife (Billie Burke), do everything possible to make their injured guest comfortable after Dr. Bradley (George Barbier) says that his leg injury is serious and he must be confined to a wheelchair. Resigned to being an unwanted guest, Whiteside decides to amuse himself by rearranging everyone's life. He turns his charm on the servants and the Stanley children (Elisabeth Fraser and Russell Arms) advising them to run away and live their own lives. By promising to cast her in a play that Katherine Cornell is dying to do, he entices glamorous actress Lorraine Sheldon (Ann Sheridan) to desert the English nobleman who is keeping her in luxury in Palm Beach and come to Ohio and break up a romance between Maggie and a local newspaper editor (Richard Travis). But, when Maggie gets wise to his scheme and threatens to resign, he ships Lorraine to a Philadelphia museum in an Egyptian mummy case presented to him by the Khedive. He is also gifted with four penguins from Admiral Byrd and an octopus from William Beebe. Once the enginery of his schemes is in motion and he must remain in the Stanley home to follow it through, Whiteside learns from Dr. Bradley there is nothing wrong with his leg; the diagnosis was a mistake. Hearing this, Whiteside bribes the doctor into silence by hinting he is affluent enough to have the physician's memoirs published.

Whiteside completes his invasion by arranging to make his annual Christmas broadcast from the Stanley home. Technicians, a boys' choir and a radio crew invade the premises. But, when Stanley discovers Whiteside's du-

plicity in feigning illness, he orders him out and suppresses his children's plan for independence.

Ready to vacate, Whiteside recognizes Stanley's eccentric sister Harriet (Ruth Vivian) as a former axe murderess who has been acquitted of hacking her parents to pieces after a family tiff. Blackmailing Stanley, Whiteside, again in command, sends the children on their way and patches up Maggie's broken romance. As he steps from the house, he slips on the icy pavement and breaks his leg. As he's carried back inside, he's told that Eleanor Roosevelt is on the telephone and wants to talk to him.

What the critics said about
THE MAN WHO CAME TO DINNER

Bosley Crowther in *The New York Times:*

Unquestionably the most vicious but hilarious catclawing exhibition ever put on the screen, a deliciously wicked character portrait and a helter-skelter satire, withal. . . .

Mr. Woolley makes *The Man Who Came to Dinner* a rare old goat. His zest for rascality is delightful. . . . One palm should be handed Bette Davis for accepting the secondary role of the secretary, and another palm should be

handed her for playing it so moderately and well. Ann Sheridan, too, as an actress of definitely feline breed, gives a tartly remembered performance.

In *Variety:*

One of the most welcome comedies of the season. . . . Monty Woolley is even better than he was in the Broadway version. . . . Bette Davis has, if anything, built up her star stature by accepting the secondary part.

NOTE: Although Chester Clute and Laura Hope Crews receive screen billing in *The Man Who Came to Dinner*, both were edited out of the final, released version.

With Ann Sheridan

With Ann Sheridan, Richard Travis, and Monty Woolley

114

IN THIS OUR LIFE

A Warner Brothers First National Picture (1942)

Cast Bette Davis, Olivia de Havilland, George Brent, Dennis Morgan, Charles Coburn, Frank Craven, Billie Burke, Hattie McDaniel, Lee Patrick, Mary Servoss, Ernest Anderson, William B. Davidson, Edward Fielding, John Hamilton, William Forest, Lee Phelps.

Credits Produced by Hal B. Wallis in association with David Lewis. Directed by John Huston. Screen play by Howard Koch. Based on the novel by Ellen Glasgow. Photographed by Ernest Haller. Musical score by Max Steiner. Musical direction by Leo F. Forbstein. Gowns by Orry-Kelly. Art direction by Robert Haas. Edited by William Holmes. Running time, 97 minutes.

Synopsis Stanley Timberlake (Bette Davis), the selfish and spoiled daughter of a genteel but impoverished Virginia family, is accustomed to having her wishes satisfied. Her mother Lavinia (Billie Burke), a bedridden neurotic, encourages Stanley to get what she wants while constantly complaining that Asa (Frank Craven), her husband, is ineffectual. Lavinia points with pride to her wealthy brother, William Fitzroy (Charles Coburn), a ruthless but successful bachelor who has an unnatural affection for his niece Stanley.

Three days before she is to marry handsome Craig Fleming (George Brent), a successful attorney, Stanley runs off with her brother-in-law, Peter Kingsmill (Dennis Morgan), a promising surgeon. Roy (Olivia de Havilland), her heartbroken sister, divorces Peter so he can marry Stanley. Roy turns to Craig in her grief and their mutual unhappiness culminates in a deep love. Stanley's marriage to Peter, who realizes his mistake too late, ends in tragedy; he commits suicide.

Returning home, a somewhat less than grieving widow, Stanley is forgiven by Roy and her family. When she learns Roy is in love with Craig, whom she threw over for Peter, Stanley cuts her mourning period short and makes an obvious attempt to win him back.

Firmly refusing to yield to Stanley's wiles, Craig fails to keep a date with her. Infuriated, Stanley drives away from the roadhouse at high speed and runs down a woman and a child—killing the child—and drives away without stopping to investigate.

Witnesses identify her car but when questioned by the police, she insists she had been home all evening on the night of the accident and had given her car to the cook's son, Parry (Ernest Anderson), to wash. The boy is arrested but his mother (Hattie McDaniel) swears he was home at the time of the accident. Roy believes her and asks Craig to handle Parry's case.

Uncovering proof of Stanley's guilt, Craig confronts her and asks her to make a confession. She refuses and goes to her Uncle William, certain he will help her. Just

With George Brent, Olivia de Havilland, Frank Craven, and Billie Burke

informed he has only weeks to live, Uncle William shows no interest in Stanley's dilemma but prevails upon her to stay with him during his last days. Realizing he is suggesting an incestuous relationship, Stanley reviles him and rushes from the house.

She drives off at a high speed and is pursued by a patrol car. Trying to outdistance her pursuers, she skids around a blind curve on the highway and crashes off the road. The car overturns and she is killed instantly.

What one critic said about
IN THIS OUR LIFE

Bob Wagner in *Script*:

Such optimistic souls as believed that Bette Davis' success with a relatively normal role in *The Man Who Came to Dinner* presaged a permanent filmic discharge from the neurological lists, are doomed to disappointment. The actress converts *In This Our Life* into an excuse to have a complete relapse and, with frenetic gaiety, packs her customary tricks into a capacious Gladstone before hieing herself on another dancing tour with St. Vitus.

Considering the extensive acclaim vouchsafed Miss Davis' past histrionic excesses, it is no small wonder that the lady favors assignments which permit her to bug her eyes, twitch her hands and maneuver the lower extremities as though in performance of some esoteric Charleston. Unfortunately, Stanley Timberlake, as conceived in the Ellen Glasgow novel, provides no legitimate reasons for theatrical hanky-panky. Nothing daunted, the star promptly dismembered the character, reassembled it in the image and likeness of many of her past portrayals. In so doing, the integrity of the Glasgow work disappears. . . .

Most of the cast members seem ill at ease; possibly they are aghast at appearing in a photoplay which proffers the premise that Bette Davis is a wench so physically en-

ticing as to be just so much cantharides to anything in trousers.

NOTE: As a gag and a good-luck gesture, members of the cast of John Huston's *The Maltese Falcon* made unbilled guest appearances in the roadhouse sequence of *In This Our Life*. Walter Huston is most recognizable as the bartender but you have to be quick to catch Humphrey Bogart, Mary Astor, Sydney Greenstreet, Peter Lorre, Ward Bond, Barton MacLane and Elisha Cook, Jr. as bar customers in the same sequence.

With Charles Coburn

With Dennis Morgan

With Olivia de Havilland

NOW, VOYAGER

A Warner Brothers First National Picture (1942)

Cast Bette Davis, Paul Henreid, Claude Rains, Gladys Cooper, Bonita Granville, Ilka Chase, John Loder, Lee Patrick, Franklin Pangborn, Katherine Alexander, James Rennie, Mary Wickes, Janis Wilson, Frank Puglia, Michael Ames, Charles Drake, David Clyde.

Credits Produced by Hal B. Wallis. Directed by Irving Rapper. Screen play by Casey Robinson. Based on the novel by Olive Higgins Prouty. Photographed by Sol Polito. Musical score by Max Steiner. Musical direction by Leo F. Forbstein. Gowns by Orry-Kelly. Art direction by Robert Haas. Edited by Warren Low. Running time, 118 minutes.

With Ilka Chase

With Claude Rains

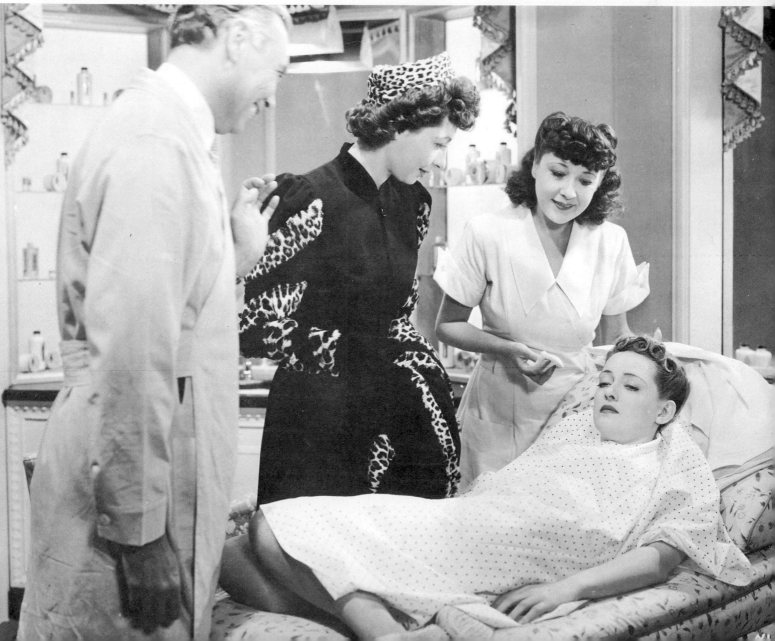

With Gladys Cooper

With Ilka Chase and Bonita Granville

Synopsis Charlotte Vale (Bette Davis), the repressed daughter of a dominating Back Bay matron (Gladys Cooper), is on the verge of a nervous breakdown because of her mother's failure to give her love and affection. Fearful for Charlotte's sanity, Lisa Vale (Ilka Chase), her sophisticated sister-in-law, brings Dr. Jaquith (Claude Rains), a famous psychiatrist, to see her. Gaining her confidence and realizing her condition is most serious, he recommends a long rest at his sanitarium. Her mother opposes such an arrangement until Lisa's fears for Charlotte's mental health are confirmed by Dr. Jaquith.

At the rest home, Charlotte undergoes analysis and therapy and learns to stand on her own feet and face the world. In three months she is transformed from an ugly spinster into a chic and attractive woman of great compassion. With Lisa's help, Dr. Jaquith arranges for her to go on a South American cruise.

During the voyage she meets Jerry Durrence (Paul Henreid), a romantic stranger whom she learns has an unloving wife who uses poor health as an excuse to hold him. While sightseeing in Rio, they are stranded overnight and in the morning find their ship has sailed. While spending the weekend together, Charlotte, hopelessly in love with Jerry, realizes he can never divorce his wife and marry her. Determined not to see him again, she returns to Boston for a frosty reunion with her hostile mother.

Lisa introduces her to Elliott Livingston (John Loder), a socialite, who asks her to marry him. Encountering Jerry accidentally, Charlotte discovers she still loves him. When her mother hears she has broken her engagement to Elliott, they have a bitter quarrel. She dies after a heart attack and Charlotte, riddled with guilt feelings, takes refuge at Dr. Jaquith's retreat where she meets Tina Durrence (Janis Wilson), Jerry's depressed and unwanted daughter.

Her heart goes out to the little girl and she implores Dr. Jaquith to allow her to help Tina feel wanted. Understanding the situation between Charlotte and Jerry, he agrees to let them go on a camping trip. Tina develops a strong attachment for Charlotte and blossoms.

When Jerry meets Charlotte again, it is at her home in Boston where he sees his transformed daughter living a normal life. Knowing his love for Charlotte can never be fulfilled, he agrees to leave Tina with her and they part once again. This time he is heartened by Charlotte's philosophy: "Don't ask for the moon when we have the stars."

With Paul Henreid and Franklyn Pangborn

With Paul Henreid

What the critics said about
NOW, VOYAGER

In *National Board of Review* magazine:

The story is more sentimental than the true psychological study it might have been. But Miss Davis is always interesting to watch and the role affords her many opportunities for fine acting. She makes the film worthwhile artistically, and gives it a dignity not fully warranted by the script.

With Paul Henreid

In *Variety:*

Bette Davis is a perfect choice for the role of a neurotic, unwanted daughter of an aged mother, turning in a moving performance filled with warmth and color to catch audience sympathy. Irving Rapper again marks himself as a director with an understanding for searching, human drama, capturing the sweep of emotion that distinguished the Olive Higgins Prouty novel. Casey Robinson displays his craftsmanship in the screen adaptation for another of his top writing jobs.

With Paul Henreid

With Ilka Chase and John Loder

With Paul Henreid

WATCH ON THE RHINE

A Warner Brothers First National Picture (1943)

Cast Bette Davis, Paul Lukas, Geraldine Fitzgerald, Lucile Watson, Beulah Bondi, George Coulouris, Donald Woods, Henry Daniell, Donald Buka, Eric Roberts, Janis Wilson, Mary Young, Kurt Katch, Erwin Kalser, Clyde Fillmore, Robert O. Davis, Frank Wilson, Clarence Muse, Anthony Caruso, Howard Hickman, Elvira Curci, Creighton Hale, Alan Hale, Jr.

Credits Produced by Hal B. Wallis. Directed by Herman Shumlin. Screen play by Dashiell Hammett. Additional scenes and dialogue by Lillian Hellman. Based on the play by Lillian Hellman. Photographed by Merritt Gerstad and Hal Mohr. Musical score by Max Steiner. Musical direction by Leo F. Forbstein. Gowns by Orry-Kelly. Art direction by Carl Jules Weyl. Edited by Rudi Fehr. Running time, 114 minutes.

Synopsis As Sara Muller (Bette Davis) crosses the border into the U.S. from Mexico with her husband and their three children to begin a long train ride to her home in Washington, D.C., Fanny Farrelly (Lucile Watson), her mother, prepares her home for the event. She hasn't seen Sara since she married Kurt Muller (Paul Lukas) eighteen years ago and went to live in Europe. Having never seen her grandchildren—Joshua (Donald Buka), Bodo (Eric Roberts) and Babette (Janis Wilson)—Fanny's anticipation is absolute. She confides her anxiety to her housekeeper, Anise (Beulah Bondi), her son David (Donald Woods) and her house guests, Count Teck de Brancovis (George Coulouris), a penurious Roumanian nobleman, and his lovely American wife, Marthe (Geraldine Fitzgerald).

When the excitement of Sara's homecoming abates, Sara tells Fanny and David that Kurt has been ill but that, when he regains his health, he will return to Europe. She evades Fanny's probing questions by saying Kurt's work as an engineer necessitated their changing addresses so often. Count de Brancovis, also curious about Kurt, forces his attaché case open and finds a large sum of American currency in it.

During a poker game at the German Embassy, where he is regarded as a parasite, the Count learns that Max Freidank, leader of an anti-Nazi underground movement, has been captured by the Gestapo but cannot be tortured into revealing the names of other members of his organ-

With Paul Lukas

ization. Rightly suspecting Kurt Muller is Freidank's right-hand man, he bargains with a German intelligence agent (Kurt Katch) to sell this information.

Confronting Kurt, the Count demands $10,000 to remain silent. Appalled by his blackmail attempt, Marthe denounces him but he silences her with accusations that she and David are having an affair. When Kurt refuses to give him the money he has collected from people interested in fighting fascism, Fanny and David offer him money. But Kurt, knowing the Count will double-cross him, is forced to shoot him.

Sara arranges Kurt's flight to Mexico and implores Fanny and David to allow him time to get away before reporting the Count's murder to the police. Realizing Kurt's importance, and his greatness, they agree. Kurt bids his family a tender farewell and leaves for Germany where, through bribery, he hopes to effect Freidank's release.

Months pass and when no word of Kurt's safe arrival comes, Sara knows that her oldest son, Joshua, will soon be going to Germany to carry on his father's work in the underground movement.

What the critics said about
WATCH ON THE RHINE

Howard Barnes in the *New York Herald Tribune*:

Watch on the Rhine is well worth seeing again whether or not you saw it during its distinguished run on the stage. It is an imperative assignment for show-going, if you missed the theatrical presentation. This time the cinema has borrowed wisely from its venerable parent and has done a terrific job on its own account in changing over a fine production to a new medium.

Bosley Crowther in *The New York Times*:

It is the first Hollywood film to go deeply into the fundamental nature of fascism. And it is the first fiction film which says bluntly some very unpleasant things which should be said. . . . And it also reveals with shocking impact the unforgivable carelessness of those who are morally opposed to fascism but who do nothing positive to check it. . . .

As a matter of fact, the magnificence of Miss Hellman's drama lies in the fortitude and compassion of her leading characters. The hero, played by Paul Lukas, is as fine a man as films have ever shown and his wife, played by Bette Davis, is a model of human selflessness.

In *National Board of Review* magazine:

No one need have feared, if anyone did, that Lillian Hellman's play would lose its point in the time that has passed since it first reached the stage. The shake-up among the magnolias—the knowledge in an American home of how far-reaching the war was even before it hit us—is no old story yet. In fact it has not been told before, and time has only ripened its meanings.

It is a fine play—and upon the screen it is still a fine play. . . . Paul Lukas here has a chance to be indisputably the fine actor he has always shown plenty of signs of being. . . . Bette Davis subdues herself to a secondary role almost with an air of gratitude for being able at last to be uncomplicatedly decent and admirable. It's not a very colorful performance, but quiet loyalty and restrained heroism do not furnish many outlets for histrionic show, and Miss Davis is artist enough not to throw in any extra bits of it to prove that she is one of the stars.

With Donald Woods and Lucile Watson

With George Colouris, Donald Woods, Lucile Watson, and Paul Lukas

THANK YOUR LUCKY STARS

A Warner Brothers First National Picture (1943)

Cast Dennis Morgan, Joan Leslie, Edward Everett Horton, S.Z. Sakall, Richard Lane, Ruth Donnelly, Don Wilson, Henry Armetta, Joyce Reynolds.

Guest Stars Humphrey Bogart, Eddie Cantor, Bette Davis, Olivia de Havilland, Errol Flynn, John Garfield, Ida Lupino, Ann Sheridan, Dinah Shore, Alexis Smith, Jack Carson, Alan Hale, George Tobias, Hattie McDaniel, Willie Best, Spike Jones and His City Slickers.

Credits Produced by Mark Hellinger. Directed by David Butler. Screen play by Norman Panama, Melvin Frank and James V. Kern. Based on a story by Everett Freeman and Arthur Schwartz. Photographed by Arthur Edeson. Music and lyrics by Arthur Schwartz and Frank Loesser. Musical direction by Leo F. Forbstein. Dances created and staged by LeRoy Prinz. Gowns by Milo Anderson. Art direction by Anton Grot and Leo Kuter. Edited by Irene Morra. Running time, 124 minutes.

Synopsis While scouting for talent for a Cavalcade of Stars benefit, two zany producers (S.Z. Sakall and Edward Everett Horton) become involved with an unknown songwriter (Joan Leslie) and a singer (Dennis Morgan) who eventually have their talents showcased on a wartime charity program featuring the following acts:

"Thank Your Lucky Stars," sung by Dinah Shore.
"How Sweet You Are," sung by Dinah Shore.
"The Dreamer," sung by Dinah Shore.
"The Dreamer," a reprise, sung and danced by Olivia de Havilland, Ida Lupino and George Tobias.
"Love Isn't Born," sung by Ann Sheridan.
"Ridin' For a Fall," sung by Dennis Morgan and Joan Leslie.
"Good Night, Good Neighbor," sung by Dennis Morgan, dance by Alexis Smith.
"Ice Cold Katie," sung and danced by Hattie McDaniel and Willie Best.
"Goin' North," sung and danced by Jack Carson and Alan Hale.
"They're Either Too Young or Too Old," sung and danced by Bette Davis.

"That's What You Jolly Well Get," sung by Errol Flynn.
"No You, No Me," sung by Dennis Morgan and Joan Leslie.
"We're Staying Home Tonight," sung by Eddie Cantor.
"Blues in the Night," parody sung by John Garfield.

What one critic said about
THANK YOUR LUCKY STARS

James Agee in *The Nation:*

Thank Your Lucky Stars is the loudest and most vulgar of the current musicals. It is also the most fun, if you are amused when show people kid their own idiom, and if you find a cruel-compassionate sort of interest in watching amateurs like Bette Davis do what they can with a song.

OLD ACQUAINTANCE

A Warner Brothers First National Picture (1943)

With Philip Reed and Dolores Moran

Cast Bette Davis, Miriam Hopkins, Gig Young, John Loder, Dolores Moran, Phillip Reed, Roscoe Karns, Anne Revere, Esther Dale, Ann Codee, Joseph Crehan, Pierre Watkin, Marjorie Hoshelle, George Lessey, Ann Doran, Leona Maricle, Francine Rufo.

Credits Produced by Henry Blanke. Directed by Vincent Sherman. Screen play by John Van Druten and Leonore Coffee. Based on the play by John Van Druten. Photographed by Sol Polito. Musical score by Franz Waxman. Musical direction by Leo F. Forbstein. Gowns by Orry-Kelly. Art direction by John Hughes. Edited by Terry Morse. Running time, 110 minutes.

Synopsis Kit Marlowe (Bette Davis), author of a sensitive best-seller, returns to her hometown as the house guest of Mille Drake (Miriam Hopkins), her friend since childhood. Although happily married and expecting a child, Millie's secret jealousy of Kit's success results in her writing a soap-opera novel which, through Kit's intervention, is published and becomes a best-seller.

Millie's success sparks her to continue writing and for a decade she produces a continuous flow of popular potboilers while Kit dedicates her talent to worthwhile creations. Wealth and fame turn Millie's head and she alienates her husband, Preston (John Loder), who leaves her after he has declared his love to Kit, who rejects his proposal of marriage.

Ten years later, during World War II, Kit encounters Preston again, an Army Major intending to be married before being shipped overseas. She wishes him happiness and mentions her engagement to Rudd Kendall (Gig Young), a Naval officer ten years her junior.

With Miriam Hopkins (on right)

With Miriam Hopkins

With Miriam Hopkins

With Esther Dale and Miriam Hopkins

Hearing that Preston is in New York, Millie invites him to visit her, hoping to effect a reconciliation. But, when she learns of his forthcoming marriage and the fact that he was once in love with Kit, she reviles her friend with charges of husband-stealing. Fed up with her selfishness, Kit shakes the daylights out of Millie and walks out on her.

Later, during the night of Millie's great revelation, Kit learns that Deirdre (Dolores Moran), Millie's beautiful daughter, is in love with Rudd, who shares her feelings. Kit suggests they get married immediately and she tells Rudd she is relieved to be free of him because she feared their marriage would never work out.

Kit goes to see Millie to bring her news of Deidre's happiness and finds her friend has made a miraculous recovery from her mental depression. So much so that she intends writing an autobiographical novel about her great friendship with Kit. Approving of this project, Kit suggests they drink a toast to the book's success and the prospect of facing middle age together.

With John Loder

What the critics said about
OLD ACQUAINTANCE

In *Hollywood Reporter:*

The sort of romantic drama often featured in women's slick paper magazines, that has always pleased the Davis public and proved financially successful. . . . Miss Davis is ever the brilliant star but, in some respects, Miss Hopkins has the better acting assignment and takes every advantage of the intentionally unpleasant character of her role.

James Agee in *The Nation:*

Miss Davis is noble enough and Miss Hopkins ignoble enough to make it unnecessary for any housewife to take the morality play personally, beyond comfortably checking on what she knew already, that virtue's peculiar rewards are hardly worth the candle. The odd thing is that the two ladies and Vincent Sherman, directing, make the whole business look fairly intelligent, detailed, and plausible; and that on the screen such trash can seem, even, mature and adventurous.

MR. SKEFFINGTON

A Warner Brothers First National Picture (1944)

With Claude Rains

Cast Bette Davis, Claude Rains, Walter Abel, Richard Waring, George Coulouris, Marjorie Riordan, Robert Shayne, John Alexander, Jerome Cowan, Johnny Mitchell, Dorothy Peterson, Peter Whitney, Bill Kennedy, Tom Stevenson, Halliwell Hobbes, Bunny Sunshine, Gigi Perreau, Dolores Gray, Walter Kingsford, Molly Lamont.

Credits Produced by Philip G. and Julius J. Epstein. Directed by Vincent Sherman. Screen play by Philip G. and Julius J. Epstein. Based on the story by "Elizabeth." Photographed by Ernest Haller. Musical score by Franz Waxman. Musical direction by Leo F. Forbstein. Costumes by Orry-Kelly. Art direction by Robert Haas. Edited by Ralph Dawson. Running time, 145 minutes.

With Claude Rains

Synopsis Fanny Trellis (Bette Davis), the reigning New York beauty, receives an unexpected visit from Job Skeffington (Claude Rains), a financial wizard, who tells her that Trippy (Richard Waring), her irresponsible brother, has been embezzling money from

With Claude Rains

the Skeffington bank where he is employed and using it to pay his gambling debts. Financially unable to pay the shortages in her brother's accounts, Fanny captures Job's affection and marries him to save Trippy from being prosecuted and sent to jail. Indignant because she married Skeffington, Trippy joins the British Air Corps and is killed in action during World War I.

Blaming Job for Trippy's death, Fanny is inconsolable and her pregnancy only adds to her grief. When the war ends, Fanny and Job, long estranged, divorce and he gives her a large cash settlement. Because her growing daughter is a constant reminder of advancing age, Fanny agrees she should live in Europe with her father. Throughout her marriage, Fanny continued to receive and entertain admirers and once free, her parade of lovers increases.

At the outbreak of World War II, Job sends young Fanny (Marjorie Riordan), now eighteen, home to her mother whose latest affair is with Johnny Mitchell (Johnny Mitchell), a young engineer. While sailing with Johnny, Fanny contracts diphtheria and almost dies. When she recovers, her fabulous beauty is gone and even her hair has fallen out. Resorting to cosmetic artifices, she tries to remain beautiful but she's faced with the overwhelming truth that she's old and dilapidated. Her vanity receives an additional blow when her daughter marries Johnny Mitchell and goes to live with him on the West Coast. Alone and ugly, Fanny faces a grim future.

One day her cousin George (Walter Abel), her lifelong counselor, tells her that Job, a victim of Nazi anti-Semitism, has returned from Europe penniless. Refusing to see

With Dorothy Peterson

With Walter Abel and Richard Waring

him because she is no longer beautiful, she changes her mind when George implores her to do one unselfish thing in her life. Seeing Job again, and discovering he is blind, she rushes to him and takes him in her arms, promising she will devote her life to looking after him. Unaware of Fanny's deterioration, Job tells her she will always be beautiful to him.

What the critics said about
MR. SKEFFINGTON

Edwin Schallert in the *Los Angeles Times:*

The mimics will have more fun than a box of monkeys imitating Bette Davis as Fanny Skeffington, née Trellis.

Excellently portraying a light selfish woman in her latest feature, the Academy Award-winning actress of other years attains as definite a characterization as she has ever proffered.

It is just the kind of enactment to inveigle the travesty specialists.

James Agee in *The Nation:*

It is another of those pictures in which Bette Davis demonstrates the horrors of egocentricity on a marathonic scale; it takes her just short of thirty years' living and two and a half hours' playing time to learn, from her patient husband (Claude Rains), that "a woman is beautiful only when she is loved" and to prove this to an audience which, I fear, will be made up mainly of unloved and not easily lovable women. Miss Davis, Director Vincent Sherman, and several others put a great deal of hard work and some that is good into this show, and there are some expert bits of middle-teens and 1920s New York atmosphere. But essentially *Mr. Skeffington* is just a super soap opera, or an endless woman's-page meditation on What To Do When Beauty Fades. The implied advice is dismaying: hang on to your husband, who alone will stay by you then, and count yourself blessed if, like Mr. Rains in his old age, he is blinded.

With Marjorie Riordan

HOLLYWOOD CANTEEN

A Warner Brothers First National Picture (1944)

Cast Joan Leslie, Robert Hutton, Janis Paige, Dane Clark, Richard Erdman, James Flavin, Joan Winfield, Jonathan Hale, Rudolph Friml, Jr., Bill Manning, Larry Thompson, Mell Schubert, Walden Boyle, Steve Richards.

Guest Stars The Andrews Sisters, Jack Benny, Joe E. Brown, Eddie Cantor, Kitty Carlisle, Jack Carson, Joan Crawford, Helmut Dantine, Bette Davis, Faye Emerson, Victor Francen, John Garfield, Sydney Greenstreet, Alan Hale, Paul Henreid, Andrea King, Peter Lorre, Ida Lupino, Irene Manning, Nora Martin, Joan McCracken, Dolores Moran, Dennis Morgan, Eleanor Parker, William Prince, Joyce Reynolds, John Ridgely, Roy Rogers and Trigger, S.Z. Sakall, Alexis Smith, Zachary Scott, Barbara Stanwyck, Craig Stevens, Joseph Szigeti, Donald Woods, Jane Wyman, Jimmy Dorsey and His Band, Carmen Cavallaro and His Orchestra, Rosario and Antonio, Sons Of The Pioneers, Virginia Patton, Lynne Baggett, Betty Alexander, Julie Bishop, Robert Shayne, Johnny Mitchell, John Sheridan, Colleen Townsend, Angela Green, Paul Brooke, Marianne O'Brien, Dorothy Malone, Bill Kennedy.

Credits Produced by Alex Gottlieb. Directed by Delmer Daves. Screen play and original story by Delmer Daves. Photographed by Bert Glennon. Musical adaptation by Ray Heindorf. Musical direction by Leo F. Forbstein. Musical numbers created and directed by LeRoy Prinz. Wardrobe by Milo Anderson. Art direction by Leo Kuter. Edited by Christian Nyby. Running time, 124 minutes.

Synopsis Slim (Robert Hutton) and Sergeant (Dane Clark), two soldiers on sick leave, spend three adventurous nights at the Hollywood Canteen before being returned to active duty in New Guinea. Slim, the millionth G.I. to enter the Canteen, wins a date with movie star Joan Leslie and Sergeant dances with Joan Crawford. They hear Canteen President Bette Davis and Vice-President John Garfield deliver a quick review of the Canteen's history, and enjoy the following musical entertainments:

"You Can Always Tell a Yank," sung by Dennis Morgan and Joe E. Brown.

"The General Jumped at Dawn," sung by the Golden Gate Quartet.

"Tumblin' Tumbleweeds," sung by the Sons Of The Pioneers.

"What Are You Doin' the Rest of Your Life?" sung by Jane Wyman and Jack Carson.

"We're Having A Baby," sung by Eddie Cantor and Nora Martin.

"Don't Fence Me In," sung by Roy Rogers.

"Sweet Dreams, Sweetheart," sung by Kitty Carlisle.

With Robert Hutton and John Garfield

With Joseph Szigeti and Jack Benny

With John Garfield

"Gettin' Corns for My Country," sung by The Andrews Sisters.

"Ballet in Jive," danced by Joan McCracken.

"Voodoo Moon," played by Carmen Cavallaro and His Orchestra; danced by Rosario and Antonio.

"The Bee," a violin duet by Joseph Szigeti and Jack Benny.

"Slavonic Dance," a violin solo by Joseph Szigeti.

"Once to Every Heart," sung by Kitty Carlisle.

What one critic said about
HOLLYWOOD CANTEEN

Howard Barnes in the *New York Herald Tribune:*

All in all *Hollywood Canteen* is a gaudy package of variety sketches which come closer to a photograph of the canteen's activities than to a cohesive photoplay. Bette Davis presides over the place with artless and wide-eyed aplomb and John Garfield gets in a lick or two as one of the moving spirits of the organization. Call the whole thing a great big scrambled vaudeville show with enough talent to have made a dozen fine movies.

THE CORN IS GREEN

A Warner Brothers First National Picture (1945)

With John Dall

Cast Bette Davis, John Dall, Joan Lorring, Nigel Bruce, Rhys Williams, Rosalind Ivan, Mildred Dunnock, Gwyneth Hughes, Billy Roy, Thomas Louden, Arthur Shields, Leslie Vincent, Robert Regent, Tony Ellis, Elliot Dare, Robert Cherry, Gene Ross.

Credits Produced by Jack Chertok. Directed by Irving Rapper. Screen play by Casey Robinson and Frank Cavett. Based on the play by Emlyn Williams. Photographed by Sol Polito. Musical score by Max Steiner. Musical direction by Robert Vreeland. Wardrobe by Orry-Kelly. Art direction by Carl Jules Weyl. Edited by Frederick Richards. Running time, 115 minutes.

Synopsis Arriving in Glensarno, a Welsh mining town where she takes up residence in a recently inherited house, Miss Lilly Moffat (Bette Davis), an English schoolmistress, is appalled to find the miners living in squalor and ignorance. Determining to help better the lives of those boys who start to work in the coal pits at a tender age, she decides to use her modest income to support a school and to teach fundamental education to any villagers interested in availing themselves of the opportunity. Her housekeeper, Mrs. Watty (Rosalind Ivan), a reformed shoplifter who has become an activist in a militant religious group, and her strumpet daughter Bessie (Joan Lorring), believe such an idealistic project is a mistake.

Faced with prejudice and opposition, Miss Moffat proceeds and enlists the services of a local gentlewoman, Miss Ronberry (Mildred Dunnock) and a shop clerk, Mr. Jones (Rhys Williams), as assistant teachers. The Squire (Nigel Bruce), a pompous landowner who openly opposes the school because he feels it will be an economic disadvantage for his interests, refuses to lease her a building in the village that would be an ideal location. Undaunted by the Squire's decision, she converts part of her house into a classroom and announces that Miss Moffat's School is ready to start classes.

Among the students is Morgan Evans (John Dall), an insolent bully who eventually reveals a spark of genius. At a moment when she is most disheartened and ready to abandon her project, Miss Moffat is awakened to Morgan's exceptional gifts and receptive mind. Allowing nothing to dismay her, she spends the next two years teaching him all that is in his power to grasp. Teacher and pupil, embarked on the great adventure of seeking and finding knowledge, share a profound and moving experience.

With Mildred Dunnock (in cart) and Rhys Williams (at gate)

Somewhat stalemated because Miss Moffat is pushing to prepare him to compete in a scholarship examination for Oxford, Morgan rebels and, after denouncing her impersonal drive, stalks from the classroom. His night of rebellious drinking and brawling includes an encounter with Bessie Watty who, still petulant over an altercation with Miss Moffat, brazenly encourages him to seduce her.

Contrite and repentant, Morgan resumes studies but, on the day of his examination, Bessie announces to Miss Moffat that she is going to have his child. Fearing such news will upset Morgan, Miss Moffat bribes Bessie to leave the village.

Months later, after Morgan has passed his examination with first honors and is ready to leave for Oxford, Bessie returns with his child. Although feeling trapped, he believes it his duty to marry her and give his son a name. Imploring him not to throw up the opportunity to make something of his life, Miss Moffat offers to adopt the child after Bessie, admittedly not in love with Morgan, agrees to such an arrangement. Satisfied, Morgan departs for Oxford, leaving his son in Miss Moffat's capable hands.

With Joan Loring and Mildred Dunnock

With John Dall

What the critics said about
THE CORN IS GREEN

E. Arnot Robinson in *Picture Post*:

As the schoolmistress in *The Corn is Green,* only Bette Davis, I think, could have combated so successfully the obvious intention of the adaptors of the play to make frustrated sex the mainspring of the chief character's interest in the young miner. This would have pulled down the whole idea of their relationship into something much simpler and more banal—more suitable to the sillier film audiences—than the subtle interpretation she insisted on giving. Drab outwardly, the schoolmistress, in her hands, became someone consumed by inward fire, by the sheer joy of imparting knowledge. Against the satisfaction of watching that performance, it seemed to me that the Hollywood unreality of the Welsh village was pretty unimportant; nothing much mattered in the film but the impression of inexhaustible vitality under a prim exterior.

Otis L. Guernsey, Jr.
in the *New York Herald Tribune*:

The motion-picture version of *The Corn is Green* is a literal translation of the stage play. The original values in this Emlyn Williams drama of education in a Welsh mining village have been handled with the utmost respect by script writers Casey Robinson and Frank Cavett. The rude realism of the Welsh character and *mise en scenè* have been preserved for the film by Irving Rapper as director and Rhys Williams as technical adviser. With these collaborators, plus Bette Davis to give dignity to the central role among an excellent supporting cast, a fine play has been passed through the Warner Brothers studio and become a polished motion picture.

Bette Davis gives a sharp, vital interpretation of Miss Moffat. . . . By remaining true to its legitimate stage counterpart, *The Corn is Green* has emerged as a notable item of film fare, a full, ripe ear of emotion and enjoyment.

With John Dall

With Joan Loring

A STOLEN LIFE

A Warner Brothers First National Picture (1946)

Cast Bette Davis, Glenn Ford, Dane Clark, Walter Brennan, Charles Ruggles, Bruce Bennett, Peggy Knudsen, Esther Dale, Clara Blandick, Joan Winfield.

Credits Produced by Bette Davis. Directed by Curtis Bernhardt. Screen play by Catherine Turney. Adaptation by Margaret Buell Wilder. Based on the novel by Karel J. Benes. Photographed by Sol Polito and Ernest Haller. Musical score by Max Steiner. Musical direction by Leo F. Forbstein. Wardrobe by Orry-Kelly. Art direction by Robert Haas. Edited by Rudi Fehr. Running time, 109 minutes.

Synopsis Kate Bosworth (Bette Davis), an introspective young artist, meets a handsome lighthouse inspector, Bill Emerson (Glenn Ford), while spending the summer on Martha's Vineyard as the house guest of her cousin and guardian, Freddie Lindley (Charles Ruggles). Just as Kate believes she is in love with Bill and he with her, her identical twin sister, Patricia (Bette Davis), shows up at the island and becomes smitten with her sister's beau. When it is apparent to Kate that Bill prefers the vivacious sister, she steps aside and Patricia and he are married.

Determined to forget Bill and make the most of her own life, Kate returns to painting and studies technique with Karnock (Dane Clark), a cruel but brilliant artist. One day, after having seen Bill briefly and learned that he and Patricia are going to Chile where he has taken an

With Dane Clark

engineer's post, Kate returns to her apartment and tells Karnock she intends giving up her art study because she realizes she will never be more than second-rate. Retreating to Martha's Vineyard, she finds Patricia, who did not go to Chile with Bill after all.

While sailing together, Patricia and Kate are caught in a sudden storm. Patricia, washed overboard, is drowned. While trying to save her, Kate loses control of the boat and it capsizes on a reef. When she regains consciousness, she discovers that Eben Folgor (Walter Brennan), the lighthouse keeper, has mistaken her for Patricia. He tells her Bill is en route home from Chile.

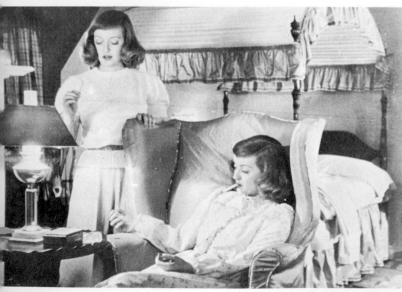

As identical twins

With Dane Clark

With Charles Ruggles and Glenn Ford (upper left)
With Walter Brennan (lower left)

With Glenn Ford (upper right)
With Glenn Ford (lower right)

Masquerading as Patricia, Kate thinks she can get away with deceiving Bill but, after learning of her sister's romantic intrigues from the maid (Joan Winfield), she returns once more to Martha's Vineyard certain she has lost Bill forever.

Realizing Patricia could never be honest with him, Bill follows her to the island, knowing that it will be Kate, the sister he should have married, who will be there.

What the critics said about
A STOLEN LIFE

Bosley Crowther in *The New York Times:*

For adult drama, incidentally, do not look to *A Stolen Life*, the new Bette Davis picture in which that lady plays the dual roles of twins. It is a distressingly empty piece of show-off for the multi-Oscar winner to perform and, at that, a quite painful presentation of the talented actress' gaits. You know there are two types of characters which Miss Davis usually plays in her films—the good girls, long-suffering and selfless, and the bad girls, inclined to spite and greed. Well, the lady here gives us both varieties, with the mechanical aid of trick photography, and the illusion is more optical than dramatic when the two are together on the screen.

In *Cue:*

A series of glib, overworked dramatic clichés that are handled as obviously and heavily as a *True Confessions* tear-jerker. The sets are too slick, the costumes too smart,

With Glenn Ford

the lines too obviously polished and pat, and the acting too superficial—for all that Bette Davis, Glenn Ford, Charles Ruggles and Walter Brennan play the leading roles. Dane Clark as a rebel modern artist has been dragged into the film for no purpose that your reporter can imagine, and was promptly forgotten.

NOTE: *A Stolen Life* was a remake of a 1939 Elisabeth Bergner film produced in Europe and released in the U.S. by Paramount.

DECEPTION

A Warner Brothers First National Picture (1946)

Cast Bette Davis, Paul Henreid, Claude Rains, John Abbott, Benson Fong, Richard Walsh, Suzi Crandall, Richard Erdman, Ross Ford, Russell Arms, Bess Flowers, Gino Cerrado, Clifton Young, Cyril Delevanti, Jane Harker.

Credits Produced by Henry Blanke. Directed by Irving Rapper. Screen play by John Collier and Joseph Than. Based on the play, *Jealousy*, by Louis Verneuil. Photographed by Ernest Haller. Musical score and Hollenius' Cello Concerto by Erich Wolfgang Korngold. Musical direction by Leo F. Forbstein. Wardrobe by Bernard Newman. Art direction by Anton Grot. Edited by Alan Crosland, Jr. Running time, 110 minutes.

Synopsis Reunited with Karel Novak (Paul Henreid), a musical genius she believed had been killed in Europe during World War II, music teacher Christine Radcliffe (Bette Davis) discovers she loves him more than ever. Bringing him to her apartment, Christine learns of his years in a concentration camp and the privations he suffered before coming to the U.S. Overcome with joy to find her unmarried, Karel expresses surprise that she can afford such a plush apartment and expensive wardrobe. Evasively, she alludes to the generosity of Alexander Hollenius (Claude Rains), a celebrated composer and conductor, who, she claims, has been her benefactor. To allay Karel's suspicion that her relationship with Hollenius has been more intimate, Christine insists they be married at once.

At their wedding reception, Hollenius appears unexpectedly and shows his obvious disapproval of Christine's marriage. Visiting him the following day, she tells him she truly loves Karel and implores him to remain silent about their former romantic attachment. Enjoying her frustration and feeling impulsively generous, Hollenius asks Karel to be solo artist at the premiere of his new cello concerto.

Elated over this opportunity for Karel to establish himself, Christine's suspicion that Hollenius' offer is less than sincere is confirmed when Karel, goaded by the maestro, gives a poor rehearsal performance that ends in a temperamental outburst. Subsequent rehearsals are equally disastrous.

Fearing Hollenius intends replacing Karel with an understudy, Christine visits him just before the concert. Thoroughly amused by her discomfort, Hollenius sug-

With Paul Henreid

With Claude Rains

gests he might ruin Karel's debut by telling him that he has been Christine's lover. Fearful that he means to do just that, Christine shoots him.

The concert is a great success and Karel's future seems assured. His triumph, however, ends on a note of tragedy when Christine confesses she killed Hollenius to prevent him from ruining Karel's chances. Disbelieving her, Karel forces her to admit the truth about her relationship with Hollenius. Aware she must account for her crime, Karel tells her that he still loves her and will do all he can to help her.

With Paul Henreid

What the critics said about
DECEPTION

In *Cue*:

The script by John Collier and Joseph Than is a masterpiece of screen writing; the performances by Bette Davis, Claude Rains and Paul Henreid are among their finest work, and the direction by Irving Rapper is faultless. Adding a rich pattern of melodic color to the play design onscreen is Erich Wolfgang Korngold's musical background, including his original 'cello concerto—a classic example of what fine screen music should be like.

Archer Winsten in the *New York Post*:

The performances are rather good. Miss Davis' in one of her standard stints, powerful emotions held on a strong rein. . . . Claude Rains, it must be admitted, goes to town with his characterization of the high-living composer and genius. If you wish to call his flamboyant measures hammy, you must add that they have quality, flavor and the so-called inner flame.

Cecelia Ager in *PM*:

It's like grand opera, only the people are thinner. . . . I wouldn't have missed it for the world.

With Paul Henreid

WINTER MEETING

A Warner Brothers First National Picture (1948)

Cast Bette Davis, Janis Paige, James Davis, John Hoyt, Florence Bates, Walter Baldwin, Ransom Sherman, Hugh Charles, George Taylor, Lois Austin, Robert Riordan, Mike Lally, Doug Carter, Harry McKee, Joe Minitello, Paul Maxey, Cedric Stevens.

Credits Produced by Henry Blanke. Directed by Bretaigne Windust. Screen play by Catherine Turney. Based on the novel by Ethel Vance. Photographed by Ernest Haller. Musical score by Max Steiner. Musical direction by Leo F. Forbstein. Art direction by Edward Carrere. Edited by Owen Marks. Running time, 104 minutes.

Synopsis Susan Grieve (Bette Davis), the daughter of a New England minister, lives alone in a plush Manhattan apartment and devotes her time to volunteer hospital work and writing socially conscious poetry that is often criticized as being sterile. At a small dinner party hosted by her friend Stacy Grant (John Hoyt) and given in honor of Slick Novak (James Davis), a naval hero, Susan feels most ill at ease when Novak dances with her cheek to cheek. Bypassing the full-blown charms of Peggy Markham (Janis Paige), his companion for the evening, Novak escorts Susan to her apartment where he is invited in for a nightcap. When the drinks are ready, Susan discovers her sudden guest has fallen asleep.

When he finally awakens, Novak apologizes for his rudeness. Susan, believing she will get rid of him quickly, is most forgiving but discovers he has no intention of leaving until after he has made romantic overtures. Unreceptive at first, she eventually succumbs to his kisses.

The following morning Novak is contrite but after breakfast Susan suggests an automobile ride in the country which eventually brings them to the Connecticut farm country where Susan owns a house she seems reluctant to visit. At Novak's insistence, they visit her farm and are greeted cordially by Mr. and Mrs. Castle (Walter Baldwin and Florence Bates), the caretakers.

After dinner Novak probes Susan's fear of the house and she tells him that it was here that her father committed suicide after her mother, Maggie McGuire, ran off with another man. Embittered by his own war experience, for which he has been decorated, and feeling he is more a coward than a hero, Novak says he intended becoming a priest but now feels unfit to serve God and the church.

Finding Novak gone the following day, Susan returns to Manhattan and reads a letter from her mother who is in a local hospital in critical condition. At Stacy's insistence, Susan meets him for dinner and they encounter Novak and Peggy who, in her moment of triumph, casts aspersions on Susan.

Novak returns to her apartment the following morning to explain that his date with Peggy was an act of defiance against falling in love with Susan. Understanding the torments that are frustrating him, Susan sends him away and advises him he should not abandon his plan to be a priest until after he makes an honest attempt to fulfill his dream. Telling him she is not bitter, she shows him her mother's letter, saying she has not only forgiven her for driving her father to suicide but that she plans to visit her. Discovering he has helped someone else learn compassion, Novak leaves with his convictions restored.

With John Hoyt

What the critics said about
WINTER MEETING

Bosley Crowther in *The New York Times*:

Of all the miserable dilemmas in which Miss Davis has been involved in her many years of movie suffering, this one is probably the worst. For it offers Miss Davis no salvation. As a neurotic spinster who falls in love with a young Navy hero whose passion, ultimately revealed, is to become a Catholic priest, it leaves her no recourse save to send her young man on his way. And that she does with such slow anguish as to make it seem interminable. Playing her agonizing boy friend is James Davis, a phlegmatic chap, who labors as much as does the film under the burden of too much talk.

In *Newsweek*:

The best that can be said for *Winter Meeting* is that its attempt to articulate Ethel Vance's obscure theme is a thoroughly honest failure, and that Bette Davis' talents are great enough to be sometimes apparent even in the midst of such unrewarding mediocrity.

Jesse Zunser in *Cue*:

Director Bretaigne Windust, an old hand at rolling conversational nothings around the Broadway stage, nudges this verbal marathon through the camera as though it were an endurance contest between director, actors and audience—which, indeed it is, with the audience as usual losing out. . . . To new leading man James Davis goes the distinction of creating a near-libelous portrait of a sailor on shore leave—a young salt who, being offered a choice of two dates, turns down a busty, steam-heated beauty on the make for an evening with a skinny, anemic and terribly cultured spinster poetess. Also, to Catherine Turney goes a wreath, probably cactus, for writing a script that is the talkiest piece of 1948.

With James Davis

With James Davis

JUNE BRIDE

A Warner Brothers First National Picture (1948)

Cast Bette Davis, Robert Montgomery, Fay Bainter, Betty Lynn, Tom Tully, Barbara Bates, Jerome Cowan, Mary Wickes, James Burke, Raymond Roe, Marjorie Bennett, Ray Montgomery, George O'Hanlon, Sandra Gould, Esther Howard, Jessie Adams, Raymond Bond, Debbie Reynolds, Alice Kelley, Patricia Northrop.

Credits Produced by Henry Blanke. Directed by Bretaigne Windust. Screen play by Ranald MacDougall. Based on the play *Feature for June* by Eileen Tighe and Graeme Lorimer. Photographed by Ted McCord. Musical score and direction by David Buttolph. Miss Davis' wardrobe by Edith Head. Art direction by Anton Grot. Edited by Owen Marks. Running time, 96 minutes.

Synopsis Much to her chagrin, Linda Gilman (Bette Davis), editor of a slick women's magazine, learns from her publisher, Carleton Towne (Jerome Cowan), that Carey Jackson (Robert Montgomery), a wandering war correspondent who once wanted to marry her, has been hired as her assistant. Aware that Carey's anti-feminist ego will make him resign his new job, Linda assigns him to a story she knows he will dislike: accompanying her and a crew to the Brinker home in Indiana where she intends doing a layout for the June issue about a wedding in a typically middle-class home.

With Robert Montgomery

Hiding his dismay, Carey assumes a flippant attitude and makes caustic comments about the efforts Linda and her assistants (Fay Bainter and Mary Wickes) put into remodeling the Brinkers, their home and the winter landscape into an image traditional for a glossy women's magazine article. The bride's mother (Marjorie Bennett) is coiffed, coutured and converted into a *cuisinière* and a chic creature unrecognizable to her family. The house is remodeled from a McKinley era monstrosity into a contemporary temple of discomfit.

Learning that the Brinkers' teenage daughter Boo (Betty Lynn) is in love with the intended groom (Raymond Roe) and that Jeanne (Barbara Bates), the bride-elect, really loves the groom's brother (Ray Montgomery) Carey sets out to straighten up the mismating. By encouraging Jeanne to elope with the brother she loves and Boo to pursue the boy she wants, Carey's efforts result in his being fired by Linda when she discovers she has no story. Once he is gone, however, Linda realizes he was right to do what he did and that what has occurred at the Brinker home is actually a better human interest story than the one she was attempting to concoct.

Back in New York with the story wrapped up, Linda encounters Carey just as he is leaving for another overseas assignment. Still in love with him and knowing he won't marry her as long as she is a career girl, she tenders her resignation and tells him she's ready to go with him and be a dutiful wife. He's disbelieving until she picks up his suitcases and tells him she intends following him like an obedient squaw wherever he goes.

What the critics said about
JUNE BRIDE

Lee Mortimer in the *New York Daily Mirror*:

The big news here is that Bette has completely discarded her well-worn crying towel. Bette Bernhardt has gone frivolous on us. . . . If for no other reason, this photoplay will forever be memorable. Not a tear. Not even a murder. And as for dramatics, none. Maybe Bette's fans won't like it, but, friends, I do! For years my dreams have been haunted by La Davis, demanding in her sternest and most tragic accents, "Philip, the letter!"

Jesse Zunser in *Cue*:

It will be welcome news that at last Bette Davis has decided to abandon the long and profitless tragic roles which for years have had her in tears and her audiences in the throes of boredom. Was a time when Miss Davis was a bright and enormously entertaining comedienne. In *June Bride* she shows she has not lost her magic touch. Together with Robert Montgomery—and with benefit of a waggish tale by Eileen Tighe and Graeme Lorimer—she helps turn this breezy comedy into one of the merriest entertainments of the movie season.

In *Liberty*:

The tragedy queen of the Warner lot wipes away the tears, gets herself done up in the new look, and has a high time of it. It's the first time she has played in a comedy in eight years, and it is one of the best performances she has ever given. . . . Pure, unadulterated fun.

With Jerome Cowan

BEYOND THE FOREST

A Warner Brothers First National Picture (1949)

Cast Bette Davis, Joseph Cotten, David Brian, Ruth Roman, Minor Watson, Dona Drake, Regis Toomey, Sarah Selby, Mary Servoss, Frances Charles, Harry Tyler, Ralph Littlefield, Creighton Hale, Joel Allen, Ann Doran.

Credits Produced by Henry Blanke. Directed by King Vidor. Screen play by Lenore Coffee. Based on the novel by Stuart Engstrand. Photographed by Robert Burks. Musical score by Max Steiner. Orchestrations by Murray Cutter. Miss Davis' Wardrobe by Edith Head. Art direction by Robert Haas. Edited by Rudi Fehr. Running time, 97 minutes.*

Synopsis Bored with life in a small Wisconsin mill town and determined to become the wife of a Chicago industrialist, Neil Latimer (David Brian), who maintains a hunting lodge near her hometown, Rosa Moline (Bette Davis) complains to her husband, Dr.

With Joseph Cotten

Lewis Moline (Joseph Cotten), that she needs a vacation far from the place where "The only decent person is the undertaker who takes you away." When Lewis is unable to finance her trip to Chicago, she intimidates his patients into paying their past due accounts. Infuriated with her, Lewis throws the few dollars at her that his patients are able to pay and tells her to go and not come back.

She meets Latimer in Chicago but he rejects her by telling her he plans to marry a socialite. Returning home to Lewis, who forgives her, Rosa resumes her routine life until Neil shows up unexpectedly and tells her he has changed his mind and now wants her to divorce Lewis and marry him.

With David Brian (upper left)
With Joseph Cotten (lower left)

With Joseph Cotten (upper right)
With David Brian (lower right)

The caretaker at Neil's lodge, Moose (Minor Watson), overhears this conversation and threatens Rosa by telling her he plans to reveal her pregnancy to Neil. Fearing Neil won't want her if he knows she is to become a mother, Rosa kills Moose during a hunting party. After a coroner's jury rules the shooting accidental, Rosa tells Lewis she is leaving him for Neil.

Lewis forbids her to go until after the baby is born. Hoping he will agree to perform an illegal operation on her, Rosa tells him that Moose's death was murder, not an accident. Lewis remains adamant, however, and he insists that Rosa have the baby. To induce a miscarriage, she jumps off a highway embankment. She loses the baby but contracts peritonitis.

While in a high-fever delirium, she gets out of bed and dresses, determined to catch the nine o'clock train to Chicago. Staggering toward the depot, she drops dead before Lewis, summoned by the maid (Dona Drake), is able to get to her. The nine o'clock express speeds on to Chicago without the midnight gal who was so determined to be on it.

With Minor Watson and David Brian

What the critics said about
BEYOND THE FOREST

In *Newsweek:*

The veteran Miss Davis makes a regrettably melodramatic mess of what is undoubtedly one of the most unfortunate stories she has ever tackled.

Dorothy Manners in the *Los Angeles Examiner:*

After 18 years and two Oscars, Bette Davis pants and rants her way out of Warner Brothers in an unforunate finale to her brilliant career there in *Beyond the Forest.*

For sheer hysteria and overexposed histrionics this is also beyond the pale. No night club caricaturist has ever turned in such a cruel imitation of the Davis mannerisms as Bette turns on herself in this one.

Arrayed in a black, Dracula-like wig, Bette snarls and gnashes her way through the role of a neurotic small town woman and succeeds in creating what is probably the most disagreeable "heroine" ever screened. This babe is a witch in spades, diamonds and clubs. . . . It is obvious that she took little direction from King Vidor, an artist well known for his restraint in directing. And the rest of the cast—all good actors—seem so dumbstruck by the antics of the star that they give the impression of merely watching from the sidelines.

Jesse Zunser in *Cue:*

In this midwestern, corn-fed version of *Madame Bovary*—in stringy hair, mascaraed eyelashes, mask-like face and a hip-swinging gait that would shame a bump-and-grind dancer—the queen of the Warner lot plays the unhappy, selfish, dissatisfied and practically psychopathic

With Minor Watson

With David Brian

wife of a poor Wisconsin country doctor. She nags, steals, cheats, and is altogether a no-good tramp who commits adultery, abortion and premeditated murder in her mad desire to get away from small-town boredom and run to Chicago. . . . The whole business is too thick to be plausible, too contrived to be convincing, too obvious in every foot of its completely foreseeable plotline. All in all, it's a little too much of everything . . . with passion steaming all over the screen.

* In some sections of the U.S., a 95-minute version of *Beyond the Forest* was shown. The sequence showing Miss Davis inducing a miscarriage was deleted.

Part Three:
ADMIRATION

On April 5, 1952, Bette Davis celebrated her forty-second birthday with a party on an RKO sound stage where, two days later, she completed her scenes in *The Story of a Divorce*, her first free-lance film after a seventeen-year tenure at Warner Brothers where she made 52 films and became known as their most valuable star. Estranged from William Grant Sherry, her third husband, she was determined not to lose her legion of admirers or her position as "First Lady of the Screen." Her last three Warner films had been less than notable and her decision to sign with Jack Skirball and Bruce Manning to star in *The Story of a Divorce* was a shrewd one. Later, released as *Payment on Demand*, it proved to be a film which gave her a chance to reassert herself. Possessed of a fine script, an excellent supporting cast and directed by Curtis Bernhardt, who had been very successful with her at Warners, the result was a first-rate film that contains one of her most worthwhile performances. Fortunately, *All About Eve*, the film she made subsequently, was released first. This re-established her as a "box-office" property.

All About Eve, notable because of Bette Davis' all-time best performance, is also one of the true classics of the screen. Bette's performance, as the aging stage star, was a canny blend of glamour, personality and acting ability. More than fifteen years after its release, *All About Eve*

is still a trenchant comedy and Bette's acting is still potent. *Payment on Demand*, a worthy follow-up, was also a substantial box-office hit and Bette was critically acclaimed for her work. The character she played in this film had many ramifications of the real Bette Davis. She was a fighter, a slightly ruthless creature determined to rise above her humble beginnings, but always a woman honest enough to admit her mistakes and to profit from them. All of her well-known mannerisms and her electric acting style are very much in evidence in this film but, rather than detract from the total sum of her effectiveness, which occasionally has happened in her films, these devices sharpened her characterization. A *tour de force* performance in a tailor-made production, to be sure, but it is also labeled with the authority of a craftsman who is something of a genius.

Bette Davis hasn't really had a great role since *Payment on Demand*, although twice—in 1952 for *The Star* and in 1962 for *What Ever Happened to Baby Jane?*—she has been nominated for an Academy Award. If anything at all can be divined from this it is conclusive proof that given half a chance she can make a good film seem great.

What Ever Happened to Baby Jane?, a curious "comedy of terrors," is deserving of a place in film history chiefly because of its immense popularity, the fact that

With Paul Henreid, director of
"Dead Ringer."

With her co-star and the children who played them
in "What Ever Happened to Baby Jane?"

she co-starred with her grand rival Joan Crawford, and its implacable proof that aging actresses can be fascinating if their talents are immutable even if their beauty is not. Oddly enough, this was not Bette Davis' first horror film. *Another Man's Poison*, an unsuccessful grotesquerie she made in England, preceded it by ten years. Also interesting, in retrospect, is the fact that she had once been assigned the feminine lead in Universal's horror classic *Frankenstein* but had been replaced by Mae Clark when producer Carl Laemmle, Jr. thought she wasn't the type of actress who should appear in horror films. But then Laemmle was also the man who thought she had no future in films.

Since making *What Ever Happened to Baby Jane?*, her career has zoomed in spite of several indifferent films and one notable exception: *Hush . . . Hush, Sweet Charlotte*, another financially successful shocker. *The Nanny*, produced in England, continues her horror cycle. And other offerings loom on the horizon.

Barbara Stanwyck, sometimes called "the poor man's Bette Davis," once said, in reference to her future as an actress, "I want to go on until they have to shoot me." This remark might very well have been made by Bette Davis, Joan Crawford, Katharine Hepburn or half a dozen other formidable stars whose careers have also been the product of their determination. Bette Davis, of course, is the champion of them all because she fought the longest for recognition, worked the hardest to maintain her success and seldom, if ever, let her public down. Her blatantly overacted performances are as memorable as her most distinguished work and her major characterizations are seared with that inextinguishable fire which burns inside of her. Without great beauty, great talent or nominal studio support, she became the most important actress of the talking screen and she made people *want* to see her.

Her career will flourish as long as she's willing to work because she has the admiration and respect of the public and the film industry itself. It's doubtful that her screen future will be as notable as her past but Miss Davis is a craftsman who knows the value of giving the public what they want. More than anything, she wants a third Academy Award. More than once, in her world, she has made the impossible possible.

Intelligent, good-humored, talented and ambitious, she has also been called ruthless, unsinkable and indestructible. She's certainly been all of these and more–much more.

With Barry Sullivan in "Payment on Demand"

As identical twins in "Dead Ringer"

147

ALL ABOUT EVE

A Twentieth Century-Fox Picture (1950)

Cast Bette Davis, Anne Baxter, George Sanders, Celeste Holm, Gary Merrill, Hugh Marlowe, Thelma Ritter, Marilyn Monroe, Gregory Ratoff, Barbara Bates, Walter Hampden, Randy Stuart, Craig Hill, Leland Harris, Claude Stroud, Eugene Borden, Steve Geray, Bess Flowers, Stanley Orr.*

Credits Produced by Darryl F. Zanuck. Screen play and direction by Joseph L. Mankiewicz. Based on the story *The Wisdom of Eve* by Mary Orr. Photographed by Milton Krasner. Musical score and direction by Alfred Newman. Art direction by Lyle Wheeler and George W. Davis. Costumes by Edith Head and Charles LeMaire. Edited by Barbara McLean. Running time, 138 minutes.

Synopsis By ingratiating herself with Margo Channing (Bette Davis), a famous and temperamental stage star she professes to admire, Eve Harrington (Anne Baxter), a girl with theatrical aspirations of her own, is hired to be Margo's secretary-companion.

Playwright Lloyd Richards (Hugh Marlowe) and Karen (Celeste Holm), his lovely wife, who have befriended the seemingly guileless Eve, give their approval to this arrangement. Only Birdie Coonan (Thelma Ritter), Margo's outspoken maid, seems to doubt Eve's sincerity.

At Margo's homecoming party for Bill Samson (Gary Merrill), the young director she hopes to marry, Eve is so superficially indispensable and so attentive to Bill that Margo, unable to contain herself, tells her off in front of her other guests: Max Fabian (Gregory Ratoff), her producer; drama critic Addison DeWitt (George Sanders); and his protégé, Miss Casswell (Marilyn Monroe). Hoping to get Eve out of her life as gracefully as possible, Margo arranges for Max to give her a job at his office. She also promises Addison DeWitt she will consider Miss Casswell as a replacement for her understudy and will read with her the following week.

Arriving too late for Miss Casswell's audition, Margo learns from Addison that Eve read in her place and has been awarded the understudy job. Furious, Margo berates Lloyd Richards and Bill for scheming behind her back. Bill, assuming Margo is jealous of Eve, walks out on her.

Karen, hearing of Margo's rudeness, decides to teach her a lesson in humility by conspiring to have her miss a performance and for Eve to take her place. The following day Addison praises Eve's performance in his newspaper column that carries an interview with Eve in which she makes some unflattering remarks about aging actresses who continue to play young girls. Bill, who re-

With Gary Merrill, Celeste Holm, and Hugh Marlowe

With Gary Merrill and Gregory Ratoff

With Marilyn Monroe and George Sanders

*With Anne Baxter, Marilyn Monroe,
and Hugh Marlowe*

*With Hugh Marlowe, Anne Baxter,
and Gary Merrill*

buffed Eve's advances the previous night, rushes to Margo with his apologies for having mistrusted her judgment of Eve.

At an intimate party celebrating Margo's engagement to Bill, Karen is approached by Eve who disclaims the statements in Addison's column. She tries blackmailing Karen into pressuring Lloyd to cast her in the leading role of his new play. Before imploring Karen to tell her what Eve had to say, Margo tells Lloyd she intends retiring and asks him to find another actress to star in his new play.

Eve, awarded the lead in Lloyd's play, tells Addison, just before the opening in New Haven, that Lloyd intends divorcing Karen and marrying her. Enlightening Eve to the fact that he is on to her schemes and knows about her sordid past, Addison tells her she belongs to him, not Lloyd.

After winning acclaim as the year's best actress, Eve returns to her hotel and finds a young girl (Barbara Bates) asleep in a chair. The girl, professing to be a great admirer of Eve's, mentions her stage aspirations. Eve, absorbed with her own triumphs, does not realize she is being taken in by a creature just like herself.

With Gary Merrill

What the critics said about
ALL ABOUT EVE

Leo Mishkin in the *New York Morning Telegraph:*

Let's get right down to cases on this. *All About Eve,* which opened at the Roxy Theater yesterday, is probably the wittiest, the most devastating, the most adult and literate motion picture ever made that had anything to do with the New York stage. It is also one of the top pictures of this year or any other recent year, a crackling, sparkling, brilliantly written and magnificently acted commentary on one of our most cherished, sophisticated and erudite institutions, the legitimate theater. And just to show you that I haven't yet run out of superlatives, *All About Eve* is also a movie in which Bette Davis gives the finest, most compelling, and the most perceptive performance she has ever played out on the screen. Including *Of Human Bondage* too. . . . You have my word for it: *All About Eve* is one of the great pictures of our time.

Alton Cook in the *New York World-Telegram:*

Bette Davis, for nearly two decades one of our greatest actresses and worst performers, finally is shaken out of her tear-jerking formula and demonstrates what a vivid, overwhelming force she possesses. She plays a fading stage star with a sardonic humor so vicious it suggests that Miss Davis must have hated that character above all others on earth. Beneath that there is also a wise understanding of the lady that leaves an audience finally idolatrous of both role and Bette.

Kate Cameron in the *New York Daily News:*

One of the outstanding screen entertainments of the year. . . . Bette has never done anything better on the screen than her playing of Margo, and the role should skyrocket her screen stock.

NOTE: In addition to Bette Davis receiving her eighth Academy Award nomination for *All About Eve,* the film still holds the all-time Academy record of 14 nominations.

* Although Eddie Fisher receives screen billing, his role—as a stage manager—was edited from the released version of *All About Eve.*

With Hugh Marlowe and Gary Merrill

With Anne Baxter, Gary Merrill, Celeste Holm, and Hugh Marlowe

PAYMENT ON DEMAND

An RKO-Radio Picture (1951)

With Barry Sullivan

Cast Bette Davis, Barry Sullivan, Jane Cowl, Kent Taylor, Betty Lynn, John Sutton, Frances Dee, Peggie Castle, Otto Kruger, Walter Sande, Brett King, Richard Anderson, Natalie Schafer, Katherine Emery, Lisa Golm, Moroni Olsen.

Credits Produced by Jack H. Skirball and Bruce Manning. Directed by Curtis Bernhardt. Screen play by Bruce Manning and Curtis Bernhardt. Photographed by Leo Tover. Musical score by Victor Young. Musical direction by C. Bakaleinikoff. Miss Davis' gowns by Edith Head. Art direction by Albert S. D'Agostino and Carroll Clark. Edited by Harry Marker. Running time, 91 minutes.

Synopsis When her husband David (Barry Sullivan), a successful corporation attorney and vice-president of a steel company, tells her he wants a divorce, Joyce Ramsey (Bette Davis), a ruthless social climber, is stunned to learn that her twenty-year marriage, which she had considered a success, is on the rocks. The following day, after David has moved to his club, Joyce is unable to keep the news of her impending divorce from her daughters, Martha (Betty Lynn) and Diana (Peggie Castle), who are sympathetic.

Reviewing her life with David from the time of their marriage and their small-town dreams up to their present social position, Joyce slowly becomes aware of the fact that her drive and ambition is what finally alienated David. But, having learned he is romantically involved with an attractive schoolteacher (Frances Dee), she threatens to countersue for divorce on the grounds of adultery unless he agrees to her property settlement. To avoid a scandal, he instructs his attorney (Moroni Olsen) to give her everything she wants. Chief among her demands are lucrative trust funds for their daughters.

Awaiting her final decree, Joyce takes a Caribbean cruise and visits Mrs. Hedges (Jane Cowl), a social crony who, divorced from her husband, has become an island recluse addicted to rum and young men. From Mrs.

With Barry Sullivan and Kent Taylor

With Barry Sullivan

151

With Walter Sande

Hedges, Joyce learns of some of the pitfalls and tragedies that face a middle-aged divorcée. A cablegram from her daughter Martha, announcing her sudden marriage, gives Joyce the excuse she needs to break off a shipboard romance with an attractive businessman (John Sutton) who admits having a wife and children.

Joyce flies home for Martha's wedding, telling her daughter not to push her husband too hard or she might lose him.

After the newlyweds leave on their honeymoon, David, who also attended the wedding reception, offers to take Joyce home. En route she tells him how lonely she has been, and unhappy that she is being divorced from the man she loves. Aware that he still loves her and realizing a part of their estrangement was his inability to resist her stratagems, he asks if she is willing to give their marriage another chance. To be certain his offer was not made out of pity, Joyce implores him to think it over and to ask her again at a later time if he still feels the same way.

With Kent Taylor and Barry Sullivan

With Jane Carol and John Sutton

With John Sutton

152

With Barbara Merrill

With David Knight

With Barry Sullivan

What the critics said about
PAYMENT ON DEMAND

In *Hollywood Reporter*:

If *Payment on Demand* has been withheld from release until the Bette Davis hit in *All About Eve* had been cemented, it wasn't necessary. The picture, completed before the 20th-Fox comedy drama, stands on its own firm feet and Miss Davis on the powerful range of her acting talent. It's a superb part and the actress plays superbly, reading nuances of the modern woman into it that her fans will recognize and understand.

Edwin Schallert in the *Los Angeles Times*:

Bette Davis puts forth one of her finest screen efforts in *Payment on Demand*, a picture which more aptly fulfills its original title, *The Story of a Divorce*. A sympathetic study of a woman's position when she seeks a legal separation from her husband in middle life, this film has many excellent attributes. . . . Miss Davis has to change character frequently during the episodes and gives an excellent account of herself in their tempestuous moments, which makes a fine contrast to her later more restrained scenes. This is no such flashy performance as she gave in *All About Eve*. It is much finer grained.

ANOTHER MAN'S POISON

An Eros Production Released by
United Artists (1952)

Cast Bette Davis, Gary Merrill, Emlyn Williams, Anthony Steele, Barbara Murray, Reginald Beckwith, Edna Morris.

Credits Produced by Douglas Fairbanks, Jr. and Daniel M. Angel. Directed by Irving Rapper. Screen play by Val Guest. Based on the play *Deadlock* by Leslie Sands. Photographed by Robert Krasker. Musical score by Paul Sawtell. Art direction by Cedric Dawe. Edited by Gordon Hales. Running time, 88 minutes. (Produced in England.)

Synopsis Celebrated mystery writer Janet Frobisher (Bette Davis), who lives in a secluded mansion on the Yorkshire moors, is in love with Larry (Anthony Steele), a young engineer engaged to marry her secretary (Barbara Murray). Having convinced him he should marry her instead, Janet is panic-stricken when her convict husband, whom she hasn't seen in years, turns up at her house and attempts to blackmail her. Fearful that he will drive Larry away, she kills him.

Later that night George Bates (Gary Merrill), another convict, shows up looking for her husband. He tells Janet that he and her husband robbed a bank that day and the police are looking for them. Unable to convince Bates that she hasn't seen her husband, she confesses to killing him after he had mistreated her. Bates helps her hide the body in a nearby lake and then announces that he intends remaining in her house and posing as her husband until the search for him quiets down.

The following day Janet is forced to tell Larry that her husband, who has been in Malaya for years, has returned and she's cornered into introducing Bates to Dr. Henderson (Emlyn Williams), the veterinarian who has been treating her horse, Fury. Curiosity aroused by the sudden appearance of a husband he didn't know existed, Dr. Henderson questions Janet's housekeeper (Edna Morris) about him but learns very little.

Because Bates' presence is encumbering her romance with Larry, Janet plots to kill him after he infuriates her by killing her horse. Sending him to the village on a fool's mission during a rainstorm, she tells him to use her jeep which she knows has faulty brakes. She's certain he'll be killed when the vehicle crashes down an incline.

Bates escapes from the accident without injury and confronts Janet with an accusation that she attempted to kill him. The following day the police start dragging the lake for the jeep and Bates tells her that her husband's

With Gary Merrill

With Anthony Steele

With Anthony Steele

What the critics said about
ANOTHER MAN'S POISON

In *Hollywood Reporter:*

The melodramatic gamut seldom has experienced the workout it is given in *Another Man's Poison*, a wild and fanciful saga. . . . Bette Davis, queen of the vixens, combs her hair, lights cartons of cigarettes, snaps her fingers and bites her consonants, and it all adds up to a performance that you'd expect to find from a night club impersonation of the actress. Plainly the director was obliged to give Miss Davis her head, for the same zealous overplaying is not evident among others in the cast. . . . Piece is plain blood and thunder, overstated in every respect.

Frank Hauser in *New Statesman and Nation:*

It is fascinating watching Bette Davis, a superb screen actress if ever there was one, play everything in a blaze of breath-taking absurdity. From beginning to end, there is not a life-like inflection, a plausible reaction. She does, in the cant phrase, The Lot, even achieving a certain grandeur in the final fade-out, which shows her laughing her life away in close-up, dosed with a blueish compound, good for horses, bad for humans; it is indeed like reading Ethel M. Dell by flashes of lightning. No one has ever accused Bette Davis of failing to rise to a good script; what this film shows is how far she can go to meet a bad one. To anyone more interested in the extremes of film standards than the workaday average other films represent, *Another Man's Poison* is not to be missed; it is safe to say there are few things in the cinema like it.

body is sure to be found. Desperate for a way out of her dilemma, Janet poisons Bates and tells Dr. Henderson he was an impostor who murdered her husband and threatened her. When Dr. Henderson tells her he knew of the impersonation and had informed the police that she was in danger, Janet faints. Attempting to revive her, Dr. Henderson feeds her some of the poisoned brandy she had used to kill Bates. Regaining consciousness, Janet, discovering what has happened and knowing she has only moments to live, laughs hysterically.

PHONE CALL FROM A STRANGER

A Twentieth Century-Fox Picture (1952)

With Warren Stevens

Cast Shelley Winters, Gary Merrill, Michael Rennie, Keenan Wynn, Evelyn Varden, Warren Stevens, Beatrice Straight, Ted Donaldson, Craig Stevens, Helen Westcott, Bette Davis, Sydney Perkins, Hugh Beaumont, Thomas Jackson, Harry Cheshire, Tom Powers, Freeman Lusk, George Eldredge, Nestor Paiva, Perdita Chandler, Genevieve Bell.

Credits Produced by Nunnally Johnson. Directed by Jean Negulesco. Screen play by Nunnally Johnson. Based on a story by I.A.R. Wylie. Photographed by Milton Krasner. Musical score by Franz Waxman. Costumes designed by Elois Jenssen. Art direction by Lyle Wheeler and J. Russell Spencer. Edited by Hugh Fowler. Running time, 96 minutes.

Synopsis While flying to Los Angeles, where he intends to start a new life and try to forget that Jane (Helen Westcott), his wife, intended deserting him and their children for another man, David Trask (Gary Merrill) comforts Binky Gay (Shelley Winters), a flashy girl passenger who admits this is her first airplane trip. Binky also expresses eagerness to see her husband Mike (Craig Stevens), whom she left when she went to New York to try out for a part she failed to get in a Broadway show. Determined to give up her dream of a stage career she says she'll make her marriage a success in spite of Sally (Evelyn Varden), her mother-in-law, a Sunset Strip night club operator who wants Mike to divorce her.

Bad weather forces the plane down at a midwestern airport where Trask is approached by another passenger, Dr. Fortness (Michael Rennie), who, having learned Trask is an attorney, seeks to have him legally represent him in Los Angeles where he intends confessing to the district attorney that he had been responsible for the death of three people in an automobile collision while

With Warren Stevens

With Gary Merrill

drunk. Dr. Fortness tells Trask he must clear his conscience so he can face his son, Jerry (Ted Donaldson), who idolizes him but suspects the truth about the accident.

Another passenger, Eddie Hoke (Keenan Wynn), an aggressive traveling salesman with a repertoire of stale jokes, suggests that he, Binky, Trask and Dr. Fortness meet in Los Angeles sometime and have a drink together and reminisce about their delayed journey. For the sake of congeniality, the quartet exchange addresses and board their plane, which is ready to take off.

Bad weather encroaches again and the plane, lost in a dense fog, makes a crash landing in a meadow near the airport. When he regains consciousness, Trask discovers his injuries are slight but that he is the only one of the quartet who survived the crash. Instead of allowing the airline to contact the victim's families, he elects to visit them and break the tragic news.

After telling Jerry Fortness that his father had intended confessing his guilt and facing the consequences, Trask is instrumental in getting the boy to return home to his mother (Beatrice Straight) instead of running away to South America. He tells Binky's husband and her mother-in-law that Binky's death was a double tragedy because she had just been signed to star in a Broadway show. This lie deflates Sally, who has been trying to convince Mike that Binky was nothing but a talentless tramp.

At Eddie Hoke's modest home, where he had been reluctant to go, Trask meets Eddie's widow, Marie (Bette Davis), who is not the bathing beauty Eddie intimated she was, but a bedridden invalid. Anticipating his surprise, Mrs. Hoke tells him she had once left Eddie, running off with another man who subsequently deserted her when she became paralyzed after a swimming accident. Aware that Eddie had seemed obnoxious to others, she tells Trask that to her he was a loyal man who forgave her indiscretion and took her back when no one wanted her, loving and worshipping her until the day he died.

Genuinely affected by the story, Trask tells her about his wife. Mrs. Hoke implores him to telephone her and let her know he survived the crash. Convinced that forgiveness is also a part of love, Trask tells his wife, as best he can, that he is returning home to her and the children.

What the critics said about
PHONE CALL FROM A STRANGER

John L. Scott in the *Los Angeles Times*:

Whether you feel *Phone Call From a Stranger* is unreal or not, the picture has some sense, intriguing scenes and is very well acted from start to finish.

In *Time*:

A cinematic party line on which several conversations are going at once, none of them coming across very distinctly. . . . Though the plot is thick, the characterizations are thin, and the film as a whole is slack as well as slick. The cast provides some flashy play-acting, notably by Bette Davis as a bedridden paralytic.

THE STAR

A Bert E. Friedlob Production Released by
Twentieth Century-Fox (1952)

Cast Bette Davis, Sterling Hayden, Natalie Wood, Warner Anderson, Minor Watson, June Travis, Katherine Warren, Kay Riehl, Barbara Woodel, Fay Baker, Barbara Lawrence, David Alpert, Paul Frees.

Credits Produced by Bert E. Friedlob. Directed by Stuart Heisler. Screen play by Katherine Albert and Dale Eunson. Photographed by Ernest Laszlo. Musical score by Victor Young. Miss Davis' Wardrobe by Orry-Kelly. Art direction by Boris Levin. Edited by Otto Ludwig. Running time, 90 minutes.

Synopsis Margaret Elliot (Bette Davis), an Academy Award winner who was once a top Hollywood star, hasn't worked for several years. Advancing age, bad films and poor investments have led her to bankruptcy. After her personal effects are sold at public auction to satisfy her creditors, she unsuccessfully appeals to Harry Stone (Warner Anderson), her agent, for an additional loan. Also rebuffed by her ex-husband's wife, who is taking care of her twelve-year-old daughter

With Warner Anderson

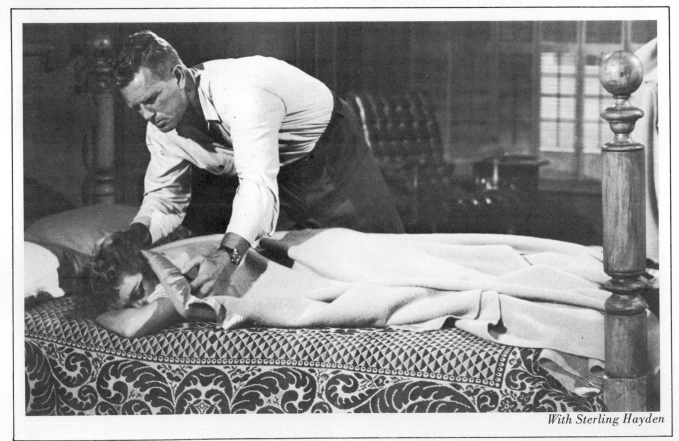

With Sterling Hayden

Gretchen (Natalie Wood), Margaret tells her lonely daughter she is negotiating for a film role which will soon make it possible for them to be together. At her modest apartment, she is confronted by her unsympathetic landlady (Katherine Warren), who insists the back rent be paid or the premises vacated.

Margaret's sister (Fay Baker) and her ineffectual brother-in-law (David Alpert), waiting inside to receive their monthly allowance, are shocked to learn she has no money, and they refuse to give her financial assistance, although she supported them for years.

Disconsolate, Margaret spends her last money on a bottle of whiskey and gets roaring drunk. Arrested, she is bailed out of jail by Jim Johannson (Sterling Hayden), an admirer who, once her leading man, now operates a boat marina where small craft are supplied and repaired. At his apartment, Jim explains his motives for paying her fine by telling her he had once been in love with her distantly. He also suggests she forget she was once a great star and that she start behaving like a woman. Certain she can make a comeback in films when her bad publicity is forgotten, she takes a saleswoman's job in a department store which terminates when she berates two customers who recognize her.

She implores Harry Stone to get her a screen test for a part in a film she always wanted to do and which is to be produced by Joe Morrison (Minor Watson). Morrison offers to test her for a supporting role in the film, and she accepts, believing that if she plays the character woman as a sexy young girl she will be awarded the top role. Days later her test is screened and as she watches her ludicrous performance, she's fully aware her glamour

days are over. Hysterical, she rushes to Harry's home where she collapses and is put to bed by his wife (June Travis).

Awakened by the noise of a party, she joins the celebration and listens while a young producer outlines a script he thinks might interest her. The story, patterned after her own life, has a moral—that an actress should never forget she must always be a woman first. Aware that she gave up the important things in her life while struggling to the top, she leaves the party and goes to Gretchen, telling her that she intends making a new life for them by marrying Jim.

At the boat marina, Jim welcomes her after she tells him she is ready to be a woman, and able to forget she has been a star.

What the critics said about
THE STAR

In *Time:*

With many scenes shot in and around Hollywood *The Star* offers some authentic behind-the-scenes glimpses of movie-town activities. Its view of its subject, however, is a rather rosily romantic one, complete with a Hollywood happy ending. Nor is the star always the grandly tragic figure she is supposed to be. But if the scripters have not made the most of their theme, Bette Davis makes the most of her role. Her performance as an ex-first lady of the screen is first-rate. . . . It is a marathon one-woman show and, all in all, proof that Bette Davis—with her strident voice, nervous stride, mobile hands and popping eyes—is still her own best imitator.

In *Newsweek:*

Bette Davis creates an acute, frightening picture of a woman obsessed with her past career and her legend, self-accusing and humble at times, but then again utterly callous to the ordinary and wonderful business of human relations. It is a fine portrait, and imparts a high value to the picture. Regrettably, there is altogether too fast and too contrived an ending to the actress's deep-seated troubles.

With Sterling Hayden

THE VIRGIN QUEEN

A Twentieth Century-Fox Picture (1955)

Cast Bette Davis, Richard Todd, Joan Collins, Jay Robinson, Herbert Marshall, Dan O'Herlihy, Robert Douglas, Romney Brent, Marjorie Hellen, Lisa Daniels, Lia Davis, Barry Bernard, Robert Adler, Noel Drayton, Iain Murray, Margery Weston, Rod Taylor, David Thursby, Arthur Gould-Peter.

Credits Produced by Charles Brackett. Directed by Henry Koster. Screen play by Harry Brown and Mindret Lord. Photographed in CinemaScope and DeLuxe Color by Charles G. Clarke. Color consultant, Leonard Doss. Musical score by Franz Waxman. Costumes by Mary Wills. Art direction by Lyle Wheeler and Leland Fuller. Edited by Robert Simpson. Running time, 92 minutes.

Synopsis On his return to England in 1581, after fighting honorably and victoriously in the Irish War, Walter Raleigh (Richard Todd) brawls his way into the favor of Lord Leicester (Herbert Marshall), a confidant of Queen Elizabeth (Bette Davis), who is so impressed with the fiery young warrior that he arranges for him to be presented at Court. Raleigh, hoping to win the Queen's attention so he can interest her in sponsoring his ambition to sail to the New World and return with great treasures, orders an expensive cloak he cannot afford so as to present a flamboyant and wealthy image at Court.

By casting his cloak across a mud puddle in the path of Queen Elizabeth as she crosses the palace courtyard, Raleigh wins her attention. Once presented to her, he takes advantage of her attraction to him to win her favor. Openly infatuated with him, Elizabeth appoints him to a post as Captain of the Guard against the advice of Chadwick (Jay Robinson), a favored counselor whose dislike of Raleigh is absolute.

Once in the Palace, and close to the Queen, Raleigh falls in love with one of her beautiful attendants, Beth Throgmorton (Joan Collins), who senses she is competing with Queen Elizabeth for Raleigh's favor. In a

With Richard Todd and Herbert Marshall

With Richard Todd and Joan Collins

position to confide in the Queen, Raleigh tells her of his hope of being sent to the New World to seek riches. Indulgent at first, Elizabeth eventually considers his offer and tells him she will commission one ship, not three, for his voyage. While awaiting her decision, Raleigh marries Beth in a secret ceremony. On the eve of his departure for the New World, Elizabeth knights him in her bedchamber. Later, when she learns he has married her lady-in-waiting, she orders his imprisonment in the Tower of London.

With Herbert Marshall

On the eve of his execution, Elizabeth visits him in his cell and tells her she had once been imprisoned there while her mother was awaiting execution. Realizing Raleigh merely trifled with her affections but certain he was sincere in his belief of the riches waiting to be claimed in the New World, she relents and sends him and his wife forth to seek gold for the coffers of England in the New World.

What one critic said about
THE VIRGIN QUEEN

Robert Downing in *Films in Review*:

Miss Davis' latest portrayal of Elizabeth I is better than her interpretation of that personage in *Elizabeth and Essex*. In *The Virgin Queen* Elizabeth is an elderly, watchful, suspicious, carping, greedy, lonely, proud, vicious and dangerous woman. Davis portrays all these human facets and royal ones as well. Her performance is a composition of shrewd intuitions about the complex sovereign who ruled an island kingdom that was being metamorphosed into an empire.

With Richard Todd

STORM CENTER

A Phoenix Production Released by
Columbia Pictures (1956)

With Alice Smith

Cast Bette Davis, Brian Keith, Kim Hunter, Paul Kelly, Kevin Coughlin, Joe Mantell, Sallie Brophy, Howard Wierum, Curtis Cooksey, Michael Raffetto, Edward Platt, Kathryn Grant, Howard Wendell, Burt Mustin, Edith Evanson.

Credits Produced by Julian Blaustein. Directed by Daniel Taradash. Screen play by Daniel Taradash and Elick Moll. Photographed by Burnett Guffey. Musical score by George Dunning. Art direction by Cary Odell. Edited by William A. Lyon. Running time, 86 minutes.

With Kim Hunter

Synopsis Alicia Hull (Bette Davis), the widow of a soldier killed in World War I, has devoted her life to public service. As librarian of the Kenport Public Library, she believes she is not merely a custodian but a guide who helps mold the future generation of her New England town. By taking a personal interest in the children and what they read, she is regarded by them as a friend and counselor. Freddie Slater (Kevin Coughlin), a boy so hungry for knowledge that he haunts the library, is her particular favorite.

With Kevin Coughlin

At a council meeting, city officials request Alicia to remove from library circulation a book, *The Communist Dream*, which they feel is subversive. Agreeing that the book is the antithesis of American ideals, Alicia, denouncing it as preposterous literature, agrees to remove it from the library shelves. Later, reviewing her hasty acquiescence, she reverses her decision and decides the book should remain in circulation. She believes its accessibility affirms the ideals of freedom. This decision results in her dismissal and the city council replaces her with Martha Lockridge (Kim Hunter), her assistant and close friend.

With Paul Kelly

Judge Robert Ellerbe (Paul Kelly), believing Alicia's firing is unfair, calls a town meeting at which he hopes

With Paul Kelly (standing)

to have her reinstated through public support. At the poorly attended meeting, Paul Duncan (Brian Keith), Martha Lockridge's fiancé and an opportunist politician, denounces Alicia and brands her a Communist because she is a member of suspect organizations. Maintaining that her interest in such organizations is because they concur with some of her ideas and not because she believes in their ideals, Alicia estranges the public and Duncan's allegations are believed.

Disturbed by Alicia's ostracism and intimidated by his playmates into denouncing her, Freddie Slater becomes so psychologically disoriented that, after a series of frenzied nightmares, he sneaks into the library and sets it on fire.

With Paul Kelly

With Howard Wierum, Paul Kelly, and Edward Platt

The citizens, seeing their library burn, are suddenly disgusted with their own fear and conservatism. The mayor (Howard Wierum), now cognizant of the council's mistake in judgment, implores Alicia to return to her job and rebuild the library. She accepts the challenge and declares the fire is partly her fault because she elected to run away rather than stand and fight for her belief that no politician should ever dictate what books a library can or cannot have.

With Paul Kelly

What the critics said about
STORM CENTER

In *Time:*

Storm Center is paved and repaved with good intentions; its heart is insistently in the right place; its leading characters are motivated by the noblest of sentiments. All that Writer-Director Taradash forgot was to provide a believable story. . . . *Storm Center* makes reading seem nearly as risky a habit as dope.

In *Cue:*

Nobody can quarrel with the justice and rightness of the theme of this film: the stupidity and threat to our culture and liberty presented by the political censorship of books, plays, films, art. But in *Storm Center* this fine dramatic idea has gone down to ignominious defeat— knocked flat on its face by a weak and silly script, bad direction, awkward performances, jerky editing, and absurd melodrama.

Daniel Taradash, who wrote the story and screenplay in collaboration with Elick Moll, and then directed the picture, is chiefly to blame for the film's disaster. The victims include, in addition to the audience, Bette Davis, Brian Keith, Kim Hunter, Paul Kelly, Joe Mantell and a screenful of supporting players.

In *Films in Review:*

. . . *Storm Center*'s script is replete with irrelevancies, changed intentions, and implausible melodrama, and is altogether synthetic. . . . Bette Davis' performance as the middle-aged librarian is adequate, but does not elicit the sympathy it should. Miss Davis' failure to win the audience is due more to the gauche things the script obliges her to do and say than to the asperity which recently has increasingly infected her performances.

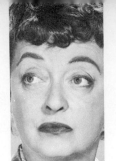

THE CATERED AFFAIR

A Metro-Goldwyn-Mayer Picture (1956)

Cast Bette Davis, Ernest Borgnine, Debbie Reynolds, Barry Fitzgerald, Rod Taylor, Robert Simon, Madge Kennedy, Dorothy Stickney, Carol Veazie, Joan Camden, Ray Stricklyn, Jay Adler, Dan Tobin, Paul Denton, Augusta Merighi, Sammy Shack, Jack Kenny, Robert Stephenson, Mae Clarke.

Credits Produced by Sam Zimbalist. Directed by Richard Brooks. Screen play by Gore Vidal. Based on the teleplay by Paddy Chayefsky. Photographed by John Alton. Musical score by Andre Previn. Art direction by Cedric Gibbons and Paul Groesse. Edited by Gene Ruggiero and Frank Santillo. Running time, 92 minutes.

Synopsis Cab driver Tom Hurley (Ernest Borgnine) returns to his Bronx apartment after a night of hacking and announces to Agnes (Bette Davis), his wife, that his dream of owning a taxicab is about to be fulfilled. At breakfast their son Eddie (Ray Stricklyn) is indifferent to this news but their daughter Jane (Debbie Reynolds) is overcome with joy. She tells her parents that she and Ralph Halloran (Rod Taylor), her fiancé, are to be married sooner than planned because they in-

With Barry Fitzgerald, Ernest Borgnine, Debbie Reynolds, and Rod Taylor

tend taking advantage of an opportunity to combine an expense-paid business trip with a honeymoon. Their wedding, in two weeks, is to be a simple affair attended only by their parents.

Hearing he will not be included in his niece's plans, Uncle Jack (Barry Fitzgerald), the Hurleys' twelve-year boarder, walks out in a huff. Telling neighbors of Jane's sudden marriage, Agnes finds them reacting suspiciously. One, Mrs. Musso (Augusta Merighi), suggests the arrangements appear to be very hasty. That night Ralph's well-to-do parents (Robert Simon and Madge Kennedy) visit the Hurleys and Mrs. Halloran smugly recalls her ability to give her daughters lavish wedding receptions. The pressure proves to be too much. Agnes, remembering her own shabby wedding, tells Jane hers will be a catered affair.

Over Jane's objections, Agnes contracts with a popular hotel to handle the reception for an estimated $2,000. Overriding Tom's objections that the money to be used would have paid for his taxicab, Agnes proceeds frivolously, reminding him they have never done much for their daughter. As the tentative guest list grows and the expenses mount, the original estimated cost is doubled. Jane's girl friend (Joan Camden) tearfully announces she cannot afford to buy a matron-of-honor gown and that her jobless husband can ill afford to rent a tuxedo. Uncle Jack, denied invitations for his barroom friends, threatens to move. Ralph, hearing the marriage must be postponed two months until the hotel can accommodate them, asks Jane to elope. When she refuses, they argue and he thinks of calling the marriage off. Asserting herself, Jane tells her mother the catered reception must be cancelled.

With Madge Kennedy, Ray Stricklyn, and Ernest Borgnine

With Ernest Borgnine

With Debbie Reynolds

Disappointed, Agnes berates Tom for failing to provide adequately for his family. In a drunken stupor, he confesses he did the best he can and he reminds Agnes that after Jane is married and Eddie is drafted they will still have to go on living with each other. Believing he failed to communicate with her, Tom falls asleep.

Jane and Ralph reunite and revert to their original wedding plans. On the day of the ceremony Tom announces to Agnes that he is taking her to the church in his new taxicab. Overcome with joy, Agnes goes off proudly with her husband, certain, for the first time, that he loves her.

What the critics said about
THE CATERED AFFAIR

Philip K. Scheuer in the *Los Angeles Times:*

The Catered Affair preserves many of the intuitive qualities that distinguished *Marty*—the ear for hidden inflections in casual words, the blurted outbursts of indignation or shame or pride, the chuckle that chokes on a tear, the incident that balloons till it bursts . . . in short, all the small, natural confusions of life and human communication. . . .Miss Davis, required to be realistic in a role that is alien to her—from the dumpy figure to the dropped g's of her speech—summoned all her admirable resources to meet the challenge. But the more she suc-

ceeded in meeting it, the more she became a triumphant Bette Davis first and a beaten Mom Hurley second.

In *The New Yorker:*

The Catered Affair which is an adaptation by Gore Vidal of a television drama by Paddy Chayefsky is a confused and wearisome account of a family squabble in the Bronx. . . . In the role of the mother, Bette Davis is done up to resemble a fat and slovenly housewife, but even so she conveys the impression that she's really a dowager doing a spot of slumming in the Bronx.

With Debbie Reynolds

With Ernest Borgnine

167

JOHN PAUL JONES

A Samuel Bronston Production Distributed by Warner Brothers (1959)

With Robert Stack

Cast Robert Stack, Marisa Pavan, Charles Coburn, Erin O'Brien, Tom Brannum, Bruce Cabot, Basil Sydney, Archie Duncan, Thomas Gomez, Judson Laure, Bob Cunningham, John Charles Farrow, Eric Pohlmann, Pepe Nieto, John Crawford, Patrick Villiers, Frank Latimore, Ford Rainey, Bruce Seaton.

Guest Stars Macdonald Carey, Jean Pierre Aumont, David Farrar, Peter Cushing, Susana Canales, Jorge Riviere, Bette Davis.

Credits Produced by Samuel Bronston. Directed by John Farrow. Screen play by John Farrow and Jesse Lasky, Jr. Photographed in Technicolor and Technirama by Michel Kelber. Musical score by Max Steiner. Costumes designed by Phyllis Dalton. Art direction by Franz Bachelin. Edited by Eda Warren. Running time, 126 minutes. (Produced in Spain.)

Synopsis Notable among the incidents in the life of John Paul Jones (Robert Stack), founder of the U.S. Navy, is one from the period following George III's (Eric Pohlmann) recognition of the United States as a sovereign state. After Jones' pleas for American sea power are denied, he goes to Russia at the invitation of Empress Catherine (Bette Davis), who has applied for a loan of his services to command Russian ships in the Black Sea.

Discovering the Empress wants him for social service instead of warfare, Jones resigns and goes to France where, seriously ill, he later dies.

THE SCAPEGOAT

A Du Maurier Guinness Production Released by
Metro-Goldwyn-Mayer (1959)

Cast Alec Guinness, Bette Davis, Nicole Maurey, Irene Worth, Pamela Brown, Annabel Bartlett, Geoffrey Keen, Noel Howlett, Peter Bull, Leslie French, Alan Web, Maria Britneva, Eddie Byrne, Alexander Archdale, Peter Sallis.

Credits Produced by Michael Balcon. Directed by Robert Hamer. Screen play by Gore Vidal and Robert Hamer. Based on the novel by Daphne du Maurier. Photographed by Paul Beeson. Musical score by Bronislau Kaper. Art direction by Elliott Scott. Edited by Jack Harris. Running time, 92 minutes. (Produced in England.)

Synopsis While on a holiday in France, John Barrett (Alec Guinness), an English professor, encounters Jacques de Gue (Alec Guinness), a Frenchman, who takes advantage of their identical appearance to carry out a murder plan in which he intends killing his wife (Irene Worth) and eloping with his mistress, Bella (Nicole Maurey), leaving everyone to believe he's really Barrett.

Tricked into carrying off a masquerade at Chateau Loire, de Gue's decaying estate, Barrett slowly uncovers details of the murder scheme. By succeeding in his impersonation, he hopes to thwart de Gue. His deception fools de Gue's mother, the Countess (Bette Davis), a bedridden dowager addicted to cigars and morphine—but not Bella.

After killing his wife in such a way that her death appears to be accidental, de Gue plans to dispose of Barrett. Trapped in a darkened room with his double, Barrett defends himself in a deadly duel.

Assuming it was de Gue who was killed and that Barrett will continue impersonating him, Bella agrees to marry him and keep his secret although she is not absolutely certain he is Barrett.

With Alec Guinness

What the critics said about
THE SCAPEGOAT

Lowell E. Redelings in the *Hollywood Citizen News*:

The story, as a whole, leaves much to be desired. On the asset side of this appraisal, the acting is commendable. Guinness is convincing in both roles. Bette Davis uses her three decades of acting experience to make the countess a commanding, and wholly believable, figure.

Louise Corbin in *Films in Review*:

The Scapegoat is good in every department of film-making except the script, which inadequately characterizes the leading parts and insufficiently motivates the major plot-turns. The acting is exceptionally good— Guinness in both parts; Bette Davis as the dope-crazed dowager countess; Nicole Maurey as the mistress; and the entire cast, which includes such fine players as Geoffrey Keen, Irene Worth and Alan Webb and such bizarre "faces" as Pamela Brown and Peter Bull.

POCKETFUL OF MIRACLES

A Franton Production Released by
United Artists (1961)

Cast Glenn Ford, Bette Davis, Hope Lange, Arthur O'Connell, Peter Falk, Thomas Mitchell, Edward Everett Horton, Mickey Shaughnessy, David Brian, Sheldon Leonard, Ann-Margret, Peter Mann, Barton MacLane, John Litel, Jerome Cowan, Jay Novello, Frank Ferguson, Willis Bouchey, Fritz Feld, Ellen Corby, Gavin Gordon, Benny Rubin, Jack Elam, Mike Mazurki, Hayden Rorke, Doodles Weaver, Paul E. Burns, George E. Stone, Snub Pollard.

Credits Produced by Frank Capra in association with Glenn Ford and Joseph Sistrom. Directed by Frank Capra. Screen play by Hal Kanter and Harry Tugend. Based on a screen play by Robert Riskin and the story *Madame La Gimp* by Damon Runyon. Photographed in Eastman Color and Panavision by Robert Bronner. Musical score and direction by Walter Scharf. Men's costumes by Walter Plunkett. Women's costumes by Edith Head. Choreography by Nick Castle. Art direction by Hal Pereira and Roland Anderson. Edited by Frank P. Keller. Running time, 136 minutes.

Synopsis Mobster Dave the Dude (Glenn Ford), who takes big chances opposing other racket czars, believes his safety is assured as long as he buys an apple each day from Apple Annie (Bette Davis), a gin-soaked peddler who has organized the Broadway beggars, as a good-luck omen. His bodyguard, Joy Boy (Peter Falk), and Junior (Mickey Shaughnessy), his chauffeur, regard his superstition as a mere idiosyncrasy but Queenie Martin (Hope Lange), his brassy, blonde moll, respects his beliefs.

Preparing to merge his enterprise with a Chicago syndicate, Dave discovers Annie has disappeared. Finding her drunk on Skid Row, he learns she is contemplating suicide because she is unable to face an impossible situation. Her daughter Louise (Ann-Margret), who has lived in a Spanish convent since infancy, is returning to New York with her fiancé (Peter Mann) and his father (Arthur O'Connell), a Spanish grandee, to meet Annie, who, Louise believes, is a socialite. Impressed by Annie's ability to support her child and carry off her deception through the mails, Dave, in a weak moment, makes a big-hearted gesture to help her. He leases a Park Avenue suite, hires a staff of servants, induces an alcoholic poli-

tician, Judge Henry Blake (Thomas Mitchell), to pose as Annie's husband and recruits Queenie and a coterie of beauty and fashion experts to convert Annie into a dowager.

The masquerade works and Louise, reunited with her mother, is assured of a large dowry by the grandee. Annie, overcome with joy, boasts that she intends giving a reception for the grandee and inviting the cream of society to meet him.

Stalling the Chicago mobster (Sheldon Leonard), who is anxious to close his merger deal, Dave rounds up a mob of hoodlums to pose as influential guests at Annie's reception. The plan backfires and Annie is ready to con-

fess the truth when, by a ruse, the governor (David Brian), the mayor (Jerome Cowan), their wives, and other dignitaries arrive at the celebration and are announced by Annie's disbelieving and imperious butler (Edward Everett Horton).

The party is a success and Louise returns to Spain with her fiancé, believing her mother to be the grandest of *grandes dames*. Dave and Queenie, having had a glimpse of respectability, consider getting married and going straight. Annie, intending to return to the streets, receives a proposal from the Judge, who considers going on the wagon.

With David Brian

What the critics said about
POCKETFUL OF MIRACLES

Wanda Hale in the *New York Daily News*:

A comedy with rowdy humor and pardonable sentiment, *Pocketful of Miracles* has Glenn Ford, Bette Davis, Hope Lang and support playing the weird, flashy Broadway characters of Damon Runyon's creation—gangsters,

With Ann-Margret, Glenn Ford, and Thomas Mitchell

molls, henchmen, panhandlers and politicians . . . the Capra comedy will create a lot of interest, beckoning those who want to see the new version of *Lady for a Day*, attracting those who want raucous humor and crackling dialogue and competent acting in their entertainment. And because it brings Bette Davis out of semi-retirement to play the ginsoaked apple peddler, Annie, which she does to our complete satisfaction.

In *Playboy*:

Frank Capra's remake of his 1933 *Lady for a Day*, whisks us back considerably more than 29 years. . . . The story has enough cracks in it for the syrup to leak through, and in the Before-After role Bette Davis slices the *jambon* in a way that will have them weeping in their lace hankies in the boondocks. Glenn Ford plays the gambler, and, as always, seems like a very nice fellow from the studio accounting department who stumbled onto the set by accident. The only first-class item in the film is Hope Lange's sharp performance as a tootsie—a happy switch from her usual, suffering, cut-off-my-arm-if-it-will-help-you parts. We'll tak' a cup o' kindness for Auld Hope Lange.

With Thomas Mitchell

WHAT EVER HAPPENED TO BABY JANE?

A Seven Arts Associates and Aldrich Production
Released by Warner Brothers (1961)

Cast Bette Davis, Joan Crawford, Victor Buono, Marjorie Bennett, Maidie Norman, Anna Lee, Barbara Merrill, Julie Allred, Gina Gillespie, Dave Willock, Ann Barton.

Credits Executive Producer, Kenneth Hyman. Associate Producer and Director, Robert Aldrich. Screen play by Lukas Heller. Based on the novel by Henry Farrell. Photographed by Ernest Haller. Musical score by Frank DeVol. Costumes by Norma Koch. Art direction by William Glasgow. Edited by Michael Luciano. Running time, 132 minutes.

Synopsis In a decaying Hollywood mansion, Jane Hudson (Bette Davis), a former child vaudeville star, and her sister Blanche (Joan Crawford), a movie queen forced into retirement after a crippling automobile accident, live in virtual isolation. Their seclusion is broken by the weekly visits of Elvira Stitt (Maidie Norman), their cleaning woman, who fears for Blanche's safety because of Jane's eccentric behavior and heavy drinking.

Learning that Blanche intends selling their home and putting her in a sanitarium, Jane reminds her sister that she is dependent on her by persecuting her in a macabre manner: serving meals consisting of roasted rats or parboiled parrots. Jane thwarts Blanche's attempts to escape from the house and deludes herself into believing she can make a theatrical comeback by reviving her old vaudeville act.

After ordering replicas of her childhood costumes, she hires Edwin Flagg (Victor Buono), a gross pianist with a mother fixation, to be her musical arranger. Aware of how ludicrous Jane's act is, Edwin feigns enthusiasm because she has promised him a large cash advance.

With Joan Crawford

With Joan Crawford

Blanche, locked in her room, attempts to escape and crawls downstairs where Jane finds her and ties her up after mistreating her unmercifully. Elvira, returning to the house after Jane has dismissed her, forces Blanche's bedroom door open and discovers Blanche bound to her bed and gagged. Jane, surprising Elvira, kills her in a moment of panic.

That night Edwin, somewhat drunk, is brought to the house by two policemen who suspect him of being a prowler. Jane corroborates his story and invites him in for a drink. While Jane entertains him, Blanche manages to upset a bedside table and he investigates the crash. Finding Blanche near death, Edwin flees from the house in a drunken stupor. Terrified that he will return with the police, Jane takes her sister to Malibu Beach where she intends burying her in the sand.

Elvira's disappearance is reported by her family. A police investigation uncovers her body and leads to a search for the missing sisters.

At dawn Blanche, close to death, confesses to Jane that she has been responsible for her mental decline because,

in a jealous rage, she had engineered the automobile accident which resulted in her injuries and had deluded Jane into thinking it was her fault.

Two motorcycle patrolmen find Jane's abandoned car nearby and as they come to arrest her, a crowd of curiosity seekers gather to watch. Jane curtsies to them and happily goes into her Baby Jane routine which had captivated audiences more than forty years before.

What the critics said about
WHAT EVER HAPPENED TO BABY JANE?

Bosley Crowther in *The New York Times*:

Joan Crawford and Bette Davis make a couple of formidable freaks in the new *What Ever Happened to Baby Jane?* But we're afraid this unique conjunction of two one-time top-ranking stars in a story about two aging sisters who were once theatrical celebrities themselves does not afford either opportunity to do more than wear grotesque costumes, make up to look like witches and chew the scenery to shreds . . . as a "chiller" of the old-fashioned type—as a straight exercise in studied horror—you may find it a fairly gripping film.

The feeble attempts that Mr. Aldrich has made to suggest the irony of two once idolized and wealthy females living in such depravity and the pathos of their deep-seated envy having brought them to this, wash out very quickly under the flood of sheer grotesquerie. There is nothing particularly moving or significant about these two.

In *The New Yorker*:

The picture is far from being a Hitchcock—it goes on and on, in a light much dimmer than necessary, and the climax, when it belatedly arrives, is a bungled, languid mingling of pursuers and pursued which put me in mind of *Last Year at Marienbad*. Still Bette Davis and Joan Crawford do get a chance to carry on like mad things, which at least one of them is supposed to be. Miss Davis has rigged herself up as an elderly alcoholic harridan of unbearable frumpy ugliness; Miss Crawford plays her sister, a comparatively well-groomed cripple, confined to a wheelchair. They've both been beauties—one a child star in vaudeville, the other a prominent movie actress—and they live now, in decayed splendor, on a side street that is plainly right off *Sunset Boulevard* . . . but don't go rummaging about Brooklyn or Queens for the picture unless you were brought up on Miss Davis and/or Miss Crawford and dote on their big, rolling eyes.

NOTE: Bette Davis received her tenth Academy Award nomination for *What Ever Happened to Baby Jane?*, the footage of which included clips from *Parachute Jumper* (1933) and *Ex-Lady* (1933), two Davis features, and also scenes from *Sadie McKee* (1934), one of Joan Crawford's MGM features.

DEAD RINGER

A Warner Brothers Picture (1964)

Cast Bette Davis, Karl Malden, Peter Lawford, Philip Carey, Jean Hagen, George Macready, Estelle Winwood, George Chandler, Mario Alcade, Cyril Delevanti, Monika Henreid, Bert Remsen, Charles Watts, Ken Lynch.

Credits Produced by William H. Wright. Directed by Paul Henreid. Screen play by Albert Beich and Oscar Millard. Based on a story by Rian James. Photographed by Ernest Haller. Musical score by Andre Previn. Costumes designed by Don Feld. Art direction by Perry Ferguson. Edited by Folmar Blangsted. Running time, 115 minutes.

Synopsis After the funeral of Frank de Lorca, her brother-in-law whom she had once loved and planned to marry, Edith Phillips (Bette Davis), a tavern owner, learns that Frank only married Margaret (Bette Davis), her identical twin sister, because he believed she was pregnant with his child. Encountering Margaret, whom she has not seen in years, Edith rejects her offers of friendship and financial help.

Resentful of Margaret's wealth and bitter because she married Frank, Edith, having learned she is about to lose her business, demands that Margaret visit her at her shabby apartment. After forcing her to admit she married Frank under false pretenses, Edith kills Margaret, changes clothes with her, and leaves her body and a suicide note in the apartment, which are found by Sgt. Jim Hobbson (Karl Malden), a Los Angeles detective, who believes the dead woman is Edith, whom he was engaged to marry.

Posing as Margaret, Edith returns to the de Lorca mansion and successfully carries off her impersonation until Tony Collins (Peter Lawford), Margaret's lover, returns from Europe and discovers the truth. Demanding

With Karl Malden

payment for his silence, he blackmails Edith into giving him some of Margaret's jewelry which he attempts to pawn. A jeweler reports this to the police and when they surreptitiously search his apartment, a cache of arsenic is found.

Confronted by Hobbson, Edith admits giving Tony the jewelry. She tells the detective he is her lover. Believing she is Margaret de Lorca, Hobbson suspects she and Tony have murdered Frank. His body is exhumed and an examination reveals he died of arsenic poisoning.

Edith, aware that Frank was murdered, confronts Tony with her knowledge. When he tries to kill her, Frank's dog, a powerful Great Dane she has befriended, comes to her rescue and kills Tony.

After she is charged with Frank's murder, Edith confesses her true identity to Hobbson but she is not believed. Convicted of Frank's murder and sentenced to be executed, Edith sees Hobbson again just before being taken to San Quentin. Admitting she lied, she tells him she really is Margaret de Lorca and not Edith, the sister he loved and wanted to marry.

With Peter Lawford

What one critic said about
DEAD RINGER

In *Time:*

Dead Ringer is predicated on the proposition that two Bette Davises are better than one. . . . Poetic justice is perhaps a bit old-fashioned but it's fun. And so is practically everything else about this trite little thriller—especially Actress Davis. Exuberantly uncorseted, her torso looks like a gunnysack full of galoshes. Coarsely cosmeticked, her face looks like a U-2 photograph of Utah. And her acting, as always, isn't really acting; it's shameless showing-off. But just try to look away.

With Peter Lawford

THE EMPTY CANVAS

A Joseph E. Levine Production Released by Embassy Pictures (1964)

Cast Bette Davis, Horst Buchholz, Catherine Spaak, Daniela Rocca, Lea Padovani, Isa Miranda, Leonida Repaci, George Wilson, Marcella Rovena, Daniela Calvino, Renato Moretti, Edorado Nevola, Jole Mauro, Mario Lanfranchi.

Credits Produced by Carlo Ponti. Directed by Damiano Damiani. Screen play by Tonino Guerra, Ugo Liberatore and Damiano Damiani. Based on a novel by Albert Moravia. Photographed by Roberto Gerardi. Musical score by Luis Enriquez Bacalov. Art direction by Carlo Egidi. Edited by Renzo Lucidi. Running time, 118 minutes.

Synopsis Dino (Horst Buchholz), the son of a dead Italian nobleman and a wealthy American woman (Bette Davis), forgets the disappointment of finding he has no talent for being a painter by succumbing to the sexual advances of Cecilia (Catherine Spaak), an amoral model who believes in indiscriminate love affairs.

Hopelessly in love, Dino takes Cecilia to a party at his mother's estate, believing she will marry him once she is convinced of his family's wealth. Unimpressed, Cecilia tells him she is willing to be his mistress until someone she likes better comes along, but she will not be his wife.

Angered by her refusal to marry him, Dino covers her nude body with banknotes. His bizarre gesture misfires when his mother accidentally interrupts their lovemaking.

Dino's mother doesn't take her son's affair seriously until Cecilia abandons him and he suffers a mental breakdown.

Seeing him through his dark days, Dino's mother feels he is fully recovered from his tragic affair when he says he's ready to resume painting and will create something worthwhile now that he has suffered and learned life is not an empty canvas.

What the critics said about
THE EMPTY CANVAS

Brendan Gill in *The New Yorker:*

The Empty Canvas is one of the worst pictures of this or any year, and more's the pity, because throughout its languid, maudlin course one catches an occasional glimpse of the *fairly* good picture it might have been. . . . The girl is an interesting character, and it's just possible that the would-be has-been of an artist and his grisly mother might also have been made into interesting characters, but the three roles have been shockingly miscast.

In *Time:*

The Empty Canvas is one of those "international" movie projects that appear to have been dreamed up by their principals (during a transatlantic jet flight?) in a spirit of reckless unity. Based on a novel by Alberto Moravia and directed by Italy's Damiano Damiani, the film stars are the U.S.'s durable Bette Davis, Germany's Horst Buchholz and Belgium's Catherine Spaak. It is chiefly notable for the fun of watching Davis breast the New Wave plot with bitchy authority.

With Horst Buchholz and Catherine Spaak

WHERE LOVE HAS GONE

A Joseph E. Levine Production Released by Paramount (1964)

Cast Susan Hayward, Bette Davis, Michael Connors, Joey Heatherton, Jane Greer, DeForest Kelley, George Macready, Anne Seymour, Willis Bouchey, Walter Reed, Ann Doran, Bartlett Robinson, Whit Bissell, Anthony Caruso, Jack Greening, Olga Sutcliffe, Howard Wendell, Colin Kenny.

Credits Produced by Joseph E. Levine. Directed by Edward Dmytryk. Screen play by John Michael Hayes. Based on the novel by Harold Robbins. Photographed in Technicolor and Techniscope by Joseph McDonald. Musical score by Walter Scharf. Costumes by Edith Head. Title song sung by Jack Jones and written by Sammy Cahn and James Van Heusen. Art direction by Hal Pereira and Walter Tyler. Edited by Frank Bracht. Running time, 114 minutes.

Synopsis As headlines announce the sordid news that his teenage daughter Danny (Joey Heatherton) has murdered his ex-wife's current lover, Luke Miller (Michael Connors) recalls his marriage to Valerie Hayden (Susan Hayward) and the subsequent events which led to this tragedy.

After attending a parade in his honor, Luke, a World War II hero, meets Valerie at a San Francisco art show where her sculpture is being exhibited. Invited to dinner by her mother, Mrs. Gerald Hayden (Bette Davis), an imperious dowager who wastes no time and few words, he is offered an executive postwar job and a large dowry as an inducement to marry Valerie. Rejecting Mrs. Hayden's offer vehemently, he stalks from her home and encounters Valerie, who tells him it is impossible for her to rebel against her mother's wishes. Admiring him for having stood up to her, Valerie falls in love with him and they marry before he returns overseas. Art critic Sam Corwin (DeForest Kelley), a former lover, predicts Valerie's marriage will end disastrously when Luke will prove incapable of satisfying her insatiable sexual desires.

After the war Luke and Valerie move into their home which has been built especially for them and furnished by Mrs. Hayden, who again implores him to work for her company. Refusing her, Luke, a talented architect with commercial ideas for low-rent housing, is determined to make it on his own. After two years of rejections from

With Susan Hayward and Michael Connors (at right)

With Michael Connors, Joey Heatherton, and Susan Hayward

bankers who refuse him financing at Mrs. Hayden's request, he accepts a vice-presidency with her company when he learns of Valerie's pregnancy.

After Danny is born, Valerie, now an acclaimed sculptress, sees Luke decline into alcoholism. Realizing he too is weak, Valerie begins running around with men who intrigue her. After Luke catches her making love to one of her muscle-man models, he walks out of her life. Mrs. Hayden arranges her divorce and Valerie, awarded custody of Danny, continues her promiscuous life until Danny is old enough to compete with her for a lover's affection.

Claiming she defended Valerie against a brutal attack,

Danny's act of murder is judged justifiable homicide and, at her custody hearing, Mrs. Hayden petitions the court to be appointed her guardian. Opposing her, Valerie confesses that Danny tried to kill her and that her lover's death was an accident resulting from his attempt to protect her. Imploring the court not to give Mrs. Hayden custody of Danny, Valerie rushes home and kills herself with a sculpting chisel. After Valerie's funeral, Luke tells Danny he will try and build a new life for her after she is released from the state institution to which she has been sentenced. He tells Mrs. Hayden that her continual interference in Valerie's life is what ultimately destroyed her.

With Michael Connors

What the critics said about
WHERE LOVE HAS GONE

In *Newsweek:*

The story is a typical Harold Robbins pastiche of newspaper clippings liberally shellacked with sentiment and glued with sex. . . . Still, Bette Davis is splendid, with her eyes rolling and her mouth working and her incredible lines to say. Sitting in the ugliest chair in Hollywood, she lowers her teacup and pronounces: "Somewhere along the line the world has lost all its standards and all its taste." . . . The foolish story seems to have been suggested by the abrupt demise of Johnny Stompanato. The gang at Embassy and Paramount, therefore, are probably congratulating themselves on their monumental restraint and good taste—simply because they didn't try to cast Lana Turner in the leading role.

Arthur Knight in the *Saturday Review:*

John Michael Hayes's script somehow manages to make every dramatic line (particularly when uttered by Susan Hayward) sound like a caption to a *New Yorker* cartoon. For badly needed compensation, however, there is Bette Davis, now grayed, matronly, and magnificent, bringing all her old verve and intensity to the role of the domineering dowager.

HUSH...
HUSH,
SWEET
CHARLOTTE

An Associates and Aldrich Production Released by
Twentieth Century-Fox (1964)

Cast Bette Davis, Olivia de Havilland, Joseph Cotten,
Agnes Moorehead, Cecil Kellaway, Victor Buono,
Mary Astor, William Campbell, Wesley Addy, Bruce
Dern, George Kennedy, Dave Willock, John Megna, Ellen
Corby, Helen Kleeb, Marianne Stewart, Frank Ferguson,
Mary Henderson, Lillian Randolph, Geraldine West, William
Walker, Idell James, Teddy Buckner and His All-
Stars.

Credits Produced and directed by Robert Aldrich.
Screen play by Henry Farrell and Lukas Heller.
Based on a story by Henry Farrell. Photographed by
Joseph Biroc. Musical score by Frank DeVol. Lyrics by
Mack David. Title song sung by Al Martino. Costumes
designed by Norma Koch. Choreography by Alex Ruiz.
Art direction by William Glasgow. Edited by Michael
Luciano. Running time, 134 minutes.

Synopsis Charlotte Hollis (Bette Davis), an aging
recluse deluded into a state of dementia by
horrible memories and hallucinations, lives in a secluded
house where, thirty-seven years before, John Mayhew
(Bruce Dern) her married lover, was beheaded and muti-
lated by an unknown assailant. Haunted by a belief that
her father (Victor Buono), now dead, had killed John
and hidden his head and hand to thwart a police investigation, Charlotte fears that the impending demolition of
her decaying home by the Louisiana Highway Commission will uncover proof of his guilt. Imploring Miriam
Deering (Olivia de Havilland), her cousin, to stop the
razing of Hollis House, Charlotte invites her for a visit.

On the night of her arrival, Miriam tells Charlotte and
Drew Bayliss (Joseph Cotten), the physician who jilted
her after the Mayhew murder, that she can do nothing to
prevent the State from tearing down the house. Late that
night, Charlotte, awakened by a lullaby played on her
harpsichord, investigates the source of the music and finds
a disembodied hand and head in the music room.

Collapsing in shock, she is put under sedation by Drew,
who tells Miriam he is gratified to see that her plan to
drive Charlotte insane and inherit control of the Hollis

With Agnes Moorehead

184

fortune is working out. The next morning Miriam discharges Velma Cruther (Agnes Moorehead), Charlotte's slovenly but faithful housekeeper, who accuses the visiting cousin of being a fortune hunter.

Velma confides her suspicions of Miriam's motives to Harry Willis (Cecil Kellaway), an insurance investigator trying to determine why Jewel Mayhew (Mary Astor), John's widow, never claimed her husband's insurance money. Finding Charlotte in a drugged stupor when she returns to Hollis House, Velma is surprised and killed by Miriam. Drew removes her body and makes her death appear to be accidental.

That night, after deluding Charlotte into believing she has killed Drew, Miriam helps her dispose of the body in a nearby bayou. Returning from her grisly mission, Charlotte encounters Drew, muddy and bloody, at the top of the stairs and she collapses into a state of animal frenzy. Later, when she regains consciousness, she sees Drew and Miriam on the terrace below her bedroom veranda and, realizing they have plotted against her, she pushes a large cement pot off its pedestal. It falls on the embracing conspirators and crushes them to death.

As Charlotte is taken into custody the following morning, a group of curiosity seekers comment on the coincidence of Jewel Mayhew's sudden death. Harry Willis, stepping from the crowd, hands Charlotte a letter in which Jewel confesses she killed John and had paid Miriam, who had proof of her guilt, to remain silent. Reading the letter while the sheriff drives her away, Charlotte, realizing the full impact of its contents, smiles ironically.

With Olivia de Havilland

What the critics said about
HUSH . . . HUSH, SWEET CHARLOTTE

Romano Tozzi in *Films in Review:*

Bette Davis and producer-director Robert Aldrich here attempt to duplicate their success with *What Ever Happened to Baby Jane?* Though not so effective as their earlier effort, this film will please all who like the macabre. *Baby Jane,* despite its contrivances, had a better story and was more believable than *Charlotte,* but the supporting cast and production values of the latter are grander.

No matter. Miss Davis, as Charlotte, gives another of her bravura performances and one which will disappoint none of her admirers.

Gene Ringgold in *Sound Stage:*

Bette Davis' 76th screen performance is as rousing as a rendition of *Seventy-Six Trombones.*

In *Time:*

Hush . . . Hush, Sweet Charlotte is a gruesome slice of shock therapy that, pointedly, is not a sequel to *What Ever Happened to Baby Jane?* The two films are blood relatives, as Producer-Director Robert Aldrich well knows, but *Charlotte* has a worse play, more gore, and enough bitchery to fill several outrageous freak shows.

Choicest holdover from *Jane* is Bette Davis, unabashedly securing her clawhold as Hollywood's *grande-dame* ghoul.

With Cecil Kellaway

THE NANNY

A Seven Arts-Hammer Film Production
Released by Twentieth Century-Fox (1965)

Cast Bette Davis, Wendy Craig, Jill Bennett, James Villiers, William Dix, Pamela Franklin, Jack Watling, Maurice Denham, Alfred Burke, Nora Gordon, Sandra Power, Harry Fowler, Angharad Aubrey.

Credits Produced by Jimmy Sangster. Directed by Seth Holt. Screen play by Jimmy Sangster. Based on the novel by Evelyn Piper. Photographed by Harry Waxman. Musical score by Richard Rodney Bennett. Wardrobe consultant, Rosemary Burrows. Edited by James Needs. Running time, 93 minutes.

With William Dix and Wendy Craig

With Wendy Craig

Synopsis Ten-year-old Joey Fane (William Dix) is due home from a school for disturbed children, where he has been undergoing treatment for two years. His father, Bill Fane (James Villiers), goes to pick him up, and is dismayed when the headmaster tells him that the youngster has been a great problem to the staff.

Back home, Joey is greeted by his mother, Virgie (Wendy Craig), and his Nanny (Bette Davis). He refuses to acknowledge Nanny, won't use the room she has made ready for him, and later, won't eat any food she has prepared.

He meets Bobbie (Pamela Franklin), the teen-age girl who lives upstairs, and tells her that his little sister Susy was drowned in the bath two years ago, that Nanny did it, but that he was blamed for it and sent away.

The following day, Virgie is taken ill with food poisoning after eating Nanny's steak and kidney pie (which Joey has been seen meddling with while Nanny was out of the kitchen). She is rushed to the hospital. Joey refuses to stay in the apartment alone with Nanny, so the doctor sends for Virgie's sister, Aunt Pen (Jill Bennett). Pen has a weak heart and must always have her medicine at hand—a fact which fascinates Joey.

As she dozes in a chair, Aunt Pen is awakened by Joey, a towel around his waist, screaming that Nanny has tried to drown him in the bath. Pen sends him to his room and goes to question Nanny, whom she discovers hovering near Joey's door with a pillow in her arms.

William Dix

A struggle for the pillow ensues, and Pen suddenly falls gasping to the floor. She begs Nanny for her medicine, but Nanny doesn't seem to hear. She carries Pen to a bedroom and places her on the bed.

As in a trance, Nanny begins to talk to the dying Pen, describing to her the events of the day on which little Susy drowned. Nanny had been alone with the children, when she received an urgent call from a doctor concerning her own grown daughter, Janet, whom she had given away when she was six months old. ("I had to, you see, because I had so many other children to look after.") Leaving Joey and Susy alone, she had gone to a squalid

With Jill Bennett

room in the slums, where she found Janet dead after an abortion. Dazed, she had walked miles through the streets of London, finally arriving home at bath time. But, as a result of her neglect, little Susy had already fallen into the tub, and was dead.

"I couldn't have Joey *tell* on his old Nanny, could I? Who would look after Madam? . . . And all those other children looked after by other Nannies—I mean, if it got out, well, parents just wouldn't trust us any more, would they?"

By now, Pen is dead. Nanny goes to Joey's room, and after a scuffle, knocks him out. She carries his body to the bathtub, which she has filled, and pushes him in and under. Suddenly, she sees not Joey but Susy in the tub, and the horror of the day two years ago comes back to her. Overwhelmed by the enormity of what she is doing, she pulls Joey from the tub and revives him. He seizes his opportunity to escape.

Now Nanny sinks slowly to her knees, all the regrets and disappointments of a lifetime sweeping over her. Weeping, she goes to her room and begins to fill her suitcase with her clothes and the framed photographs of all her "children."

What one critic said about
THE NANNY

Judith Crist in the *New York Herald Tribune:*

In this, her fourth venture into the Hitchcock-cum-horror milieu, Miss Davis is out for character rather than hoax and comes up with a beautifully controlled performance as a jealous and voracious nursemaid pitted against a wilful and obviously disturbed 10-year-old. Miss Davis sets the standard, and indeed it is her performance and four complementary ones that give this film its distinction.

191